It is delightful to see another book by Lynne Souter-Anderson, contributing to the field of Clay Therapy.

Her first book, *Touching Clay, Touching What? The Use of Clay in Therapy*, first published in 2010, gave credence and credibility to using clay in therapy. It was a pioneering book in the field of the creative arts therapies and gave a broad perspective on working in this modality with all age groups.

This new book is written for already qualified professionals who want to add the use of Clay Therapy in their work with children and adolescents.

Monika Jephcott,
Chief Executive Play Therapy UK (PTUK)

Clay is multi-faceted which allows tactile and creative expression. Therapeutically, clay offers the child and adolescent endless opportunities to express feelings, emotions and thoughts across all developmental ages and stages.

In the field of clay therapy, Lynne's contribution is significant including the '*Five Lenses of Theoretical Anchoring for Clay*' as a framework to use with this medium. This book is an extension of Lynne's work and her dedication to developing therapists' knowledge and skills in using clay within child, adolescent and adult psychotherapy.

Karen O'Neill,
Clinical Director Counselling Solutions, EMDR Europe Accredited Practitioner

Lynne's passion and knowledge for working therapeutically with clay is infectious.

She has presented clay therapy workshops to our Blue Smile Charity many times. Our therapists always leave the workshops with more confidence, new skills and further exciting ideas in how to use clay with their young clients.

Anita Gatt,
Clinical Services Manager, Blue Smile — Children's Mental Health Charity, UK

This wonderful book is an easy to digest go-to reference for those interested in the therapeutic use of clay. It is alive with case material and practical information covering some of the key issues that may arise during child and adolescent development. It certainly whets the appetite for undertaking necessary and dedicated training in this field. A marvellous achievement much deserving of re-publication.

Dr Jude Adcock,
Arts-Based Counsellor, Clay Therapist, Psychotherapist & Clinical Supervisor, Cornwall, UK

Making Meaning

Clay Therapy with Children and Adolescents

The Wisdom of the Transpersonal

Making Meaning

Clay Therapy with
Children and Adolescents

Lynne Souter-Anderson

ARCHIVE
publishing

First published in the UK in 2015 by Hinton House

This Revised Edition Published in the United Kingdom by
Archive Publishing
Shaftesbury, Dorset, England

Designed at Archive Publishing by Ian Thorp MA

A CIP catalogue record for this book is available from
The British Library

ISBN 978-1-906289-65-2 (Paperback)
ISBN 978-1-906289-73-7 (ePub)

Front cover: Clay sculpture by 8 year old Thea Carter

www.archivepublishing.co.uk

Printed and bound in England
by CMP (UK) Ltd

DEDICATION

To the memory of mother

ACKNOWLEDGEMENTS

What makes this book special is that at the heart of it are ten case studies written about clay therapy with children and adolescents. These young people showed much courage as they faced their difficulties working through therapy. It was my enormous privilege to have been part of their journey in accompanying them as they led the way and I give my heartfelt admiration and thanks to them.

I am especially indebted to Monika Jephcott, (Chief Executive, Play Therapy UK) and the late Jeff Thomas, (Systems and Communications Director of Play Therapy UK and Registrar for the Professionals Standard Association Register), for their acknowledgement of the place of clay in therapeutic work with children and adolescents and their encouragement that I write further on the subject.

I have felt tremendously supported by the warmth received from Chris Wise, Dilys Phipps, Agi Lloyd and Julie Robinson as I moved towards completing the case studies and the section elaborating the theory that underpins the practice described in the book, (see Chapter 1, Clay Therapy, 'Theoretical Under-pinning of Clay Therapy', and Appendix, 'The Theory of Contact: Physical, Emotional, Spiritual and Metaphorical'). I express my sincere gratitude to these special people.

I feel honoured by the generosity of spirit shown by five master's students who gave permission for their research studies to be included in this book. Thank you to Eileen Braham, Susannah Bradley, Caroline Drew, Donna Jones and Louise Burton.

Conversations within the Clay Therapy Community of practitioners were insightful and inspirational, and each member is especially remembered here for sharing their ideas.

Over the years, I have encountered many people fascinated with the use of clay in therapy and whose ideas, material and advice have contributed to making this publication possible. I remember here, especially Ian Thorp, of Archive Publishing, who has been an absolute stalwart in his enthusiasm for publishing the books I have written on Clay Therapy. I feel particularly indebted to Ian for his support and knowledge of the publishing world, as *Making Meaning: Clay Therapy with Children and Adolescents* required re-publishing.

My final thanks go to my hugely supportive family: to Dave, Derek, Samuel, Fran and Bonnie, Hannah, Adam, Freya, Finn Thea and Max. You all give something very special — love — which makes everything possible.

Namaste

CONTENTS

Part One: Clay Therapy

Part Three: Clay Therapy with Adolescents – Case Studies

Chapter   **page**

Part Four: Clay Therapy Initiatives

Chapter   **page**

FOREWORD

It is delightful to see another book by Lynne Souter-Anderson, contributing to the field of Clay Therapy. Her first book, *Touching Clay, Touching What?: The Use of Clay in Therapy* (2010), gave credence and credibility to using clay in therapy. It was a pioneering book in the field of the creative arts therapies and gave a broad perspective on working in this modality with all age groups.

This new book is written for already qualified professionals who want to add the use of Clay Therapy in their work with children and adolescents. It is a hands-on book for practitioners and easy to read. However, the application of clay therapy in this specialist field requires appropriate additional training.

Lynne's book is a significant addition to the small but growing library of books on the market about specialist therapeutic approaches with young children and adolescents. Play Therapy UK (PTUK)'s research analysis of over 300,000 therapeutic sessions using the 'toolkit'(sand, music, clay, art/drawing, puppets, movement, drama, therapeutic story, creative visualisation etc.) has shown that clay is the fifth most used medium in play therapy sessions. It is therefore an important medium to offer to children and adolescents to support their healing process.

Lynne achieves a good balance between the application of theory and the actual process, which is always valuable for the reader. This is especially well demonstrated in Chapter 1, 'Clay Therapy: Theoretical Underpinning of Clay Therapy', in which the author explains her own theoretical basis, 'The Theory of Contact: Physical, Emotional, Spiritual and Metaphorical'. She uses the analogy of the 'five lenses' to demonstrate the stages of immersion and discovery in the clay therapy process, and includes an invaluable diagram to clarify her theory about the evolving nature of the process.

For me the book comes really alive through the ten case

studies, which demonstrate how clay therapy has been used with the younger clients and adolescents, a client group that can prove to be difficult to reach and work with in therapy. The illustrations used deepen the experience and understanding of the process for the reader. Throughout the case studies glimpses of the quality of the therapist's presence are seen, because she has the courage to show her own process thereby offering authenticity to the work.

To be able to do this effectively specialised training is required There is still very little published in the field, but it is heartening and exciting to see recent research initiatives described in the master's dissertations produced by students at the Academy of Play and Child Psychotherapy and Cambridge University, which are included towards the end of the book.

Lynne's book is a 'must-read' for all creative play and arts therapists

Monika Jephcott
Chief Executive Play Therapy UK (PTUK)

PREFACE
(Revised Edition)

My experience of teaching pottery overlaps five decades whilst my clinical practice using the arts spans some thirty years. Continuing to integrate my interest in the arts with therapy and education, my initial research for a master's degree at the Institute for Arts and Education, Islington was designated 'An analysis of the therapeutic use of clay in a variety of settings.' This was followed by invitations to deliver workshops on the therapeutic use of clay at the Play Therapy International World Congress held in Chichester in 2004 and sessions using clay with attachment issues at the Dublin Conference in 2005.

Both events afforded the opportunity to share ideas with Monika Jephcott, President of Play Therapy International, Doctor Violet Oaklander and Sir Richard Bowlby on clay use which increased the desire to make it my life's work to promote using clay in therapy. This was followed by a time of intense focus on the value and use of clay in therapy when I became a Doctoral student in Psychotherapy at the Metanoia Institute, London.

Findings from the Doctoral research project were distilled and published in *Touching Clay: Touching What, The Use of Clay in Therapy* (2010), my first book on using clay in therapy. This seemed enthusiastically received and when practitioners requested a manuscript specifically covering clay therapy with children and adolescents I became excited at the prospect of writing again.

My aim in writing, *Making Meaning: Clay Therapy with Children and Adolescents* has been to offer contemporary perspectives on the application of working with clay in therapy sessions with a young client group. The content of this book has been drawn fully from my own experiences while delivering therapy education and in the course of clinical practice. Although there is obvious relevance to practitioners and trainees working in the arts, play and drama therapies this book essentially is of value to therapists from varied theoretical backgrounds. The intention here has been to make the modality of clay therapy readily accessible to all practitioners by deepening understanding of the process involved, whilst at the same time developing the skills repertoire for this particular client base. Another intention of this book is to offer validation to you, the practitioner seeking to work with the creative arts in settings where the environment is not so easily controlled — in that children and therapy rooms can be less predictable!

The contemporary increase of interest in the use of clay in therapy begs the question: 'Why now?' Since the discipline of counselling and psychotherapy has become a mainstream field within the mental health provision, you will most probably be aware that reliance on 'talking' therapies alone is not always the most appropriate way to help improve emotional well-being. This is particularly true when working with children and adolescents.

Clay therapy is an active therapy founded on sensate experiences; those of touch and movement, embodied encounters with matter that can help to connect us with the power of the imagination. Searching to understand and make meaning of difficult and traumatic situations and confusing experiences is possible when working with clay with children and adolescents, for the relevance of this process is something immediately grasped and understood by the young. Working in clay thus can be considered a 'universal language,' crossing language and cultural barriers.

The book is divided the book into four parts. Part One gives information on clay therapy and begins with an explanation of what this therapy involves. The new theoretical under-pinning for clay therapy I named the 'Theory of Contact: Physical, Emotional, Spiritual & Metaphorical' (Souter-Anderson, 2012), has been condensed in the last part of Chapter 1, 'Theoretical Underpinning of Clay Therapy', although I thought it worthwhile to include a detailed version in the Appendix for those

xxii MAKING MEANING: CLAY THERAPY

readers whose appetite has been wetted and who are keen to know more. The case study in Chapter 13, 'Eating Conditions', provided a valuable opportunity to illustrate and expand upon the practical application of the theory.

We then move on to descriptions of equipment, construction methods, explorations of clay creations and processes, and finally the developmental phenomena children experience when working with clay. Some aspects of the aforementioned may seem somewhat basic to you and I hope you will excuse this fact, but it seemed important to include information about equipment and construction methods because therapeutic practitioners really do want to have this knowledge when their previous experience does not include the use of clay.

The second and third parts provide glimpses of how I have used clay therapy with younger clients. I found the experience of writing these studies very emotional at times because I recalled the clinical work that took place and the courage the children and adolescents showed in working through their worries. Ten case studies; five involving children from five years to eleven years old and five covering adolescent therapy are the heart of this book. It is noteworthy that therapy with adolescents can be tricky and yet clay seems to reach into the parts of our psyche that other modalities cannot easily access.

Basing the selection of the diverse cases on problems that frequently beset children and adolescents I decided to preface each case study with the reasons for its inclusion. This is then followed by general information on the subject of the case being presented. Background information to the specific case is included, and then we move on to consider the client response to the therapeutic intervention using clay, what they experienced while using the medium and something of the quality of my presence and way of communicating with the client. The choice to conclude with discussion points on the respective case studies hopefully offers you additional thought-provoking material to compliment your personal response to the read. All names and circumstantial details have been changed to protect client identity.

Current initiatives in the field of clay therapy are exciting, and Part Four showcases five recent dissertations by master's students. Their work is shared in the belief that they shine valuable light on the process of clay therapy, further enhancing the reader's experience. The final parts of this section offers details of the innovative clay therapy training programme that I wrote and began in 2012, which may be useful if you wish to extend your clinical knowledge.

Making Meaning: Clay Therapy with Children and Adolescents is a distinctive book that will expand knowledge, theory and practice on the fascinating use of clay in therapy with younger clients in unique ways, thereby adding to the still scant literature on the subject in a pioneering spirit.

Filled with passion for promoting clay therapy and compassion for struggling children and adolescents I hope you will find the contents of this book open the door to curiosity and inspire the use of clay further as a creative intervention within your practice.

Lynne Souter-Anderson
Cambridgeshire, 2024

PART ONE

CLAY THERAPY

Chapter 1

What is Clay Therapy?

Introducing Clay Therapy

Clay Therapy is a form of active psychotherapy during which unidentified and unexpressed feelings and emotions become visible through physical manipulation of clay. Working with clay in therapy is potentially both powerful and profound, because worries that previously have caused inner concern or turmoil are given shape and form in the outer world. When problems can be seen, it is easier to share difficulties by talking them through with a qualified practitioner in a safe environment.

Clay Therapy enables communication when problems are hard to put into words. This makes it a universal language for fostering emotional intelligence and is especially helpful when working with issues such as anger, bereavement, loss, attachment, separation, harassment, bullying, sexual identity, transgender issues, shame, and guilt. Clay therapy therefore has wide application.

How Clay Therapy Works

In a safe space, when a respectful working relationship has been created, the trained therapist invites the client to work freely with a lump or block of clay creating whatever takes shape. When talking is not required the fingers and hands, wrists, elbows or perhaps feet, make contact with the medium by simply holding, smoothing, squeezing, squashing, bashing or using some other action. This touching of earth in the form of clay frequently initiates right and left brain communication whereby forgotten ideas and buried experiences and memories are activated, bringing them more into consciousness.

Most people find touching clay is a pleasant experience and since no specific prior skills or knowledge are needed it is rare that a client experiences failure in being able to work with the medium. However, it is important for the therapist to have personal experience of working with clay to fully understand the impact this form of therapy can have.

Who Benefits from Clay Therapy?

Many clay therapists use clay to work with all age groups, from three upwards. Children and adolescents engage with clay in a purposeful way, helping them to understand upsetting and confusing experiences, enabling release of feelings. They rarely worry about making a mess. Individual adults, couples and groups also find that once they have touched the clay in a therapy session an outlet for expression has been activated. Clay is particularly useful for people from different cultural backgrounds. Likewise children, adolescents and adults with learning or physical disabilities are able to access Clay Therapy.

What is Clay?

It is valuable to have some knowledge of what clay is, so that if asked about the medium being used the therapist is able to give a brief explanation. For adults and children alike it is difficult to comprehend that the substance of clay originated from the inner core of the Earth, millions of years ago. Thinking for a moment of what this means is staggeringly powerful. The profundity of the concept is awesome: we are holding in our hands and working with a medium that has been around far longer than we can ever imagine.

It is little wonder Jung (Schwartz-Salant, ed., 1995) referred to this primal matter as *radix ipsius* (root of itself), containing, the essence of the world's soul. He links the idea of a world soul to his work on the concept of a collective unconscious, where dwell the archetypal images located in cultural myths, tales and symbols throughout the world. These images offer universal understanding and emotional and behavioural responses to human experiences. In this realm of thinking it follows that clay therapy is a close relation to sandplay therapy and can be seen as a sister therapy to sandplay therapy.

Clay and sand are different forms of earth. They both offer distinct handling experiences. In terms of a geological study sand is ground down earth, whereas clay is a primal substance that is formed from the erosion of rock. Clay is older than sand. The expression 'Grandfather Rock and Mother Earth' is frequently heard. Clay appears to connect and speak to the primal aspects of being human, whereas sandplay works on the shores of consciousness and unconsciousness.

Children are absolutely fascinated by these ideas, appearing spellbound. Without ever saying much on the subject, they understand they have a spiritual connection with clay. At a very young age there can be a closeness to archetypal energies, so when imagination is harnessed there can be movement into a marvellously rich world, that of the stream of the personal unconscious. This may lead to accessing an even deeper stream: the field of the collective unconscious, in which images of the earliest human instincts connect us with our spiritual heritage which assist in helping to structure meaning.

Geological Constitution of Clay and the Significance to Clay Therapy

It can be hard to comprehend that the very clay used in clay therapy was deposited some three million years ago. The natural energy that permeates clay is often unrecognised and yet when the therapist and client are working together there is a desire for harmonious equilibrium, the ebb-and-flow rhythm of a relationship capable of releasing calming and strengthening feelings. This can be likened to a grounding experience, during which working with clay connects us to the earth, the root of all, including human existence.

Clay cannot be described as having any particular consistency and is extremely varied in colour. It is described in many geological books as a feldspar rock that has disintegrated over millions of years. Feldspar rock is any group of hard rock-forming minerals consisting of aluminium silicates of potassium, sodium, calcium or barium. These are the primary constituents of igneous rocks (rocks derived from lava that solidified on or below the earth's surface or, alternatively from magma, a paste-like hot, viscous liquid within the earth's crust which solidifies to form igneous rock).

Sometimes igneous rocks are described as 'related to' fire. Metaphorically fire is associated with fuel and energy and this brings the concept of working with clay full circle, in that it could be said that the medium of clay holds energy and is primordial in nature. Sometimes this concept might be shared with a young client depending upon circumstances and their developmental understanding.

Theoretical Underpinning of Clay Therapy

Making meaning is a fundamental purpose of therapy, but it can be a complex and elusive procedure. Theories are guidelines to assist the therapist in gaining deeper understanding of the process through clinical discussions with colleagues and supervisors. This section describes my underpinning theory for clay therapy which I call the 'Theory of Contact: Physical, Emotional, Spiritual and Metaphorical', in which aspects of Jungian theory, object-relations theory and existential perspectives are interwoven. (Souter-Anderson, 2010)

Initially termed the 'Theory of Contact: Physical, Emotional and Metaphorical', this has since been expanded to include 'Spiritual'. The importance of acknowledging spirituality as a crucial dimension in clay therapy has been made clear in feedback from participants at conference, seminars and workshops. In these venues therapists working with clay have discussed their responses to situations in life and they often refer to ideas of spirituality. These ideas have subsequently been assimilated into my theoretical underpinning of clay therapy.

There are many complex processes involved in making these connections during clay therapy, including physical, physio-logical, biochemical, neurological, emotional and psychological. As a result, therapists generally acknowledge and appreciate that the relationship between the therapist, the client and the clay is infinitely more intricate than was initially realised.

The 'Theory of Contact; Physical, Emotional, Spiritual and Metaphorical' is best understood through a framework of five lenses, due to the continuous oscillation of fragile but powerful connections intrinsically and intricately interlinking client and therapist as they work together in clay therapy.

Lens 1: Making Contact

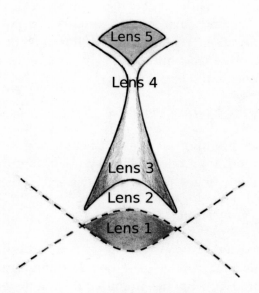

Five Lens Framework for Clay Therapy Theory
(From *Touching Clay, Touching What?*, Souter-Anderson, 2010, p. 52)

This is the stage of touching the clay physically and thereby making contact with the actual substance. If we are playing with clay, we are playing with earth and this naturally links closely to Jungian theory. According to Stevens, (1990, p. 235), '...psychologically the prima material is identical with the primal Self'.

Lens 2 – Play space of potential

Here we have the space of potential where, through touching and playing with the clay, body and mind work together as one. Movement, massage and changes in breathing can shift the neuro-chemical processes, usually taking the creator usually into altered states of consciousness.

Lens 3 – Clay play in the presence of another

As the creator plays with the clay in the presence of a therapeutic practitioner the emotional contact often contributes towards a time of exploration. What transpires through the play in the presence of another transmutes and 'vaporises' up through the conical flask image into lens 4.

Lens 4 – Bridging Space of Potential

A second space of importance is that between lens 4 and lens 5 where an alchemical process enables symbolic and metaphorical contact by actively engaging the imagination.

Lens 5 – Emerging Theme

The creating period draws to a close and, whether the outcome of this phase is a clay image or some other tangible evidence of process exploration, what has unfolded during the session often links to existential themes.

A more detailed explanation of the different lenses can be found in the Appendix.

Chapter 2.

Clay Therapy Equipment

This chapter covers the type of clay suitable for clay therapy, storage of the clay and the recycling of used clay, followed by an explanation of the basic equipment needed to get started.

Types of Clay

Natural clay comes in many different colours and types depending upon mineral content, but the most usual type to use for clay therapy is that which is referred to as 'earthenware clay' such as terracotta (red) clay or the buff (greyish) clay. The clay is often packaged in 12.5 kilo bags.

Natural clay can usually be obtained from a local studio potter or by linking up with a local secondary school or institute of further education (it may be possible to order or purchase supplies by getting to know staff in the art/ceramic department).

It is always possible to use man-made clays, in other words clay substitutes. These mediums are not as effective as clay in therapy. Whilst they have their uses and it may be helpful to make them available in the therapy room as alternatives, the texture and handling properties are not the same as those of natural clays. It is recommended that therapeutic practitioners work with man-made and natural clays on their own before taking the medium into the therapy room, because it is likely that you will develop a preference through your experience of the clays.

Man-made clays are to be found in many countries and will be known by brand names. In the United Kingdom it is possible to purchase such brands as Reinforced Newclay, Plasticine, Fimo, Sculpy and Cernit. The advantage of using these clays is that they are air-drying and therefore do not require firing in a kiln to gain hardness. This also means that they can be decorated or painted perhaps in a follow-up therapy session. The use of these clays involves introducing a different concept into clay therapy.

Storage of clay

After obtaining a supply of clay, it is advisable to store the bags in a cool place, such as a garage or concrete-built store. Always remember to keep the clay sealed in airtight bags. Should the clay bag become torn, re-bag using strong plastic or alternatively you can repair the tear with parcel tape.

Once exposed to air, the clay will begin to dry out, necessitating a recycling procedure, so it is advisable to carry out a weekly check on moistness level. Should the clay begin to dry out, sprinkle some water on the solid mass or wrap the clay in a very damp old tea-towel and carefully reseal the clay bag. Avoid leaving solid masses of clay lying in pools of water in the bags otherwise it will become a gooey mess. This would not be an absolute disaster provided the clay is not needed immediately.

Whether the clay is from a new bag or has been recycled it is helpful to cut it into different sized cubes. These can be placed in a transparent bag which sits inside a plastic lidded bucket, ready to be of use in the therapy room.

Recycling Clay

Practitioners and clients alike appreciate the idea of being eco-friendly in recycling clay so, when a lump of clay is no longer required, place it into a bucket. Cover it with just enough water to let it slake down. This helps the drier clay to change into a mud-like substance. Varied weather conditions and temperatures mean this might take three to five days or so; it is difficult to be exact. It happens when it happens!

Push your fingers into the mud-like substance in the bucket to see if the clay slurry feels soft enough to dig out by handfuls and plop onto a wooden board in small, mountain shapes. Around six hours later (note the word 'around') turn the small mountains upside down. This can be quite a messy process and therapeutic in itself to those preparing the clay! Once the small clay mountains have been exposed to the elements and excess moisture has evaporated, it is time to shape the clay into cubes by gently patting the different facets of the clay lump on the board. After the clay is shaped, remember to store in a transparent polythene bag placed in a transparent plastic lidded container ready for re-use.

Useful Equipment When Working With Clay

Very little equipment is required in order to work with clay and there is no need to spend a great deal of money to get clay therapy up and running. Below are the bare essentials of equipment you will need and a short explanation of their use.

- Wooden board
- Heavy duty plastic sheeting
- Clay cutters
- Wooden rolling pins
- Wooden slats
- Small wooden mallet
- Recycled water containers
- A few modelling tools
- Plastic containers
- Small buckets
- Old shirt/apron
- Hand wipes
- Dustpan and brush

Wooden boards

When using clay with children and adolescents, wooden boards provide a good base on which to pummel, flatten, squash, roll or rest the clay. Clients seem to appreciate choosing the board from a small stack of different sizes and thickness but generally a thinnish board (about 30 cm x 45 cm) provides is a good platform.

Old wooden chopping boards or bread boards are just as effective as are pieces of hessian or thick floor cloths. However, it is better to avoid working directly on plastic or vinyl surfaces since clay will stick to such a surface, usually interrupting the work in hand.

Heavy duty plastic sheeting

This is very useful for putting underneath the wooden boards, whether working on tables, benches or flooring and do help to minimise clearing up time.

Clay cutters

Clay cutters or wire cutters resembling cheese cutters aid the segmenting of clay into cubed portions. When buying a small set of inexpensive pottery tools from a craft store, there is usually a wire cutter included. If not, a nylon fishing line stretched taut between two small pieces of dowelling will suffice.

Wooden rolling pins

Children and adolescents alike are often eager to have a go at rolling out a lump of clay into slabs or sheets. It is helpful to keep both full-sized rolling pins and small children's rolling pins as found in baking sets. These work best when they are dry since damp rolling pins encourage the clay to stick fast to the wood!

Wooden slats

These may be cut from strips of different thicknesses of MDF and are useful when making slabs of clay. As a rule, slats of around 30 cm long are best so as not to knock everything else off the board being worked on.

Small wooden mallet

It is wonderfully physical to bash a lump of clay over and over again with a wooden mallet, thereby releasing pent-up emotions and bottled-up anger.

Recycled water bottles

It is important to have water containers in a therapy room that does not have a sink and care should be taken over ensuring the bottles are full, in order not to cause disruption to the work when in full flow.

A few modelling tools

The most significant work is created mainly through direct skin contact with the clay. But specialist clay modelling tools with ends of different shapes are easily purchased. It is also useful to have available forks, knives, spoons, biscuit cutters, old biro cases, shells, corks or screws in case the client wishes to use them.

Plastic containers

A variety of plastic containers are invaluable for making slip or slurry, when water is added to clay and mixed to make a medium with a runny consistency. Plastic vegetable trays or polystyrene tray bases for storage or the carrying of clay creations can also be useful.

Plastic buckets

Buckets should be in various sizes, with some lids, and are useful during a clay therapy session for holding the discarded clay and any dirty water.

Old shirts or aprons, hand-wipes, dustpan & brush

Old shirts or aprons will help to minimise mess on clothing although sometimes extra layers of clothing can get in the way of free flow working. Hand-wipes enable the client to wipe mess from hands and arms or feet and faces, and are particularly useful where there is no running water. A dustpan and brush helps to maintain a clean working environment.

Chapter 3

Construction Techniques

In this chapter the different basic construction techniques that can be used when working with clay will be discussed — thumb or pinch pots, tile or plaque making, slab building, coil work, sculpting and modelling plus the modelling of a human figure. There are no hard and fast rules for making clay creations, although it is always worthwhile handling the clay in a sympathetic manner if the creations are to be kept. That said, if a client is in need of bashing a piece of clay to a pulp, then any sympathetic handling can be forgotten as the anger is appropriately unleashed!

Non-Directive Use of Clay with Children

A small child has an innate need to touch. They reach out to touch a lump of clay. The clay body does not yield easily unless it is of a slip consistency so the child's curiosity is aroused. Watching small children of 2 to 3 years old working with clay is quite fascinating, for they seem to seek a response from this material that can be soft, sticky and slippery — or hard, like a rock. Of course, there are many tactile experiences between 'sticky' and 'hard' and it is those that the child wants to explore further.

Responding to a young child's sense of curiosity by being fully non-directive with clay facilitates true and free exploration. This level of freedom is wonderfully exhilarating for this is when children are learning about control and autonomy. The notion of omnipotence is what so many troubled young clients simply need act out, that is to say, they need to feel they can control life around them. A medium, such as clay that responds in its own way to being touched and moved is astonishingly obliging in enabling this.

Children from about 2 years upwards will attempt to pat, poke or pinch a lump of clay. When they realise that this material is similar to Playdoh there is a desire to make something. Naturally a young child's modelling skills are going to be quite limited and unrefined. Nevertheless, the handling of a lump of clay seems to activate the imagination. Adults as well as children and adolescents seem intrigued by clay.

Using Clay in a More Directive Approach with Adolescents

Older children and adolescents are keen to develop some skills and show prowess and ability when working with clay. In terms of chronological play and social development according to both Piaget (1962; 1971) and Erikson (1967) this is an important time when self-confidence and self-worth are becoming more established. As a result the young adolescent client is more likely to seek some technical help and guidance when attempting to construct models in clay. They might even ask the therapist what should be made. But more often than not, when hands come into contact with the clay there is not much need to respond to such a question as the impetus to be self-directed is underway.

However, when working on specific client concerns with adolescents, it is probable that the therapist will realise a little more direction may be of benefit. This kind of direction can be seen throughout the case study chapters in Part Two. At times the reader will note that a non-directive approach is adopted at the start of a session, moving seamlessly into a more directive approach as the session unfold. The case studies offer pointers on this sensitive management style for clay work sessions, especially Chapter 15, which looks at the issue of teenage depression and problems associated with relocation.

The construction of a clay image need not be restricted to one method. A mixed-method approach is often used and the different approaches have few rules, allowing imagination free rein. However, should clay creations be fired in a kiln (the process by which it is transformed from a leather-hard state to a permanently hard finish), then some guidelines should be given about how to attach pieces of clay to each other, for example, how to attach a tail to the body of a dog and how thick a model can be. As this book is not intended to be a technical guide, it can be helpful to obtain a user-friendly pottery book.

Basic Techniques

This book may not be a technical guide, but it is important to understand the meaning of a few basic techniques. An understanding of 'slip' and 'scoring' for example, will be crucial when joining pieces of clay together so that they stay together!

Slip

Slip is clay that has a runny consistency similar to double cream. This liquid clay is used for joining or bonding two pieces together. For example, when attempting to join a teddy bear's arms to the body, it is prudent to rub a little slip where the join will take place. One of the quickest and easiest ways to make slip in a therapy session is to take a small lump of clay, roll it into a sphere, push a thumb into it, add a tiny amount of water and then mix up the clay and water to make the consistency of double cream.

Scoring

Scoring is the roughening of the clay edges when two pieces are to be joined. This is done by scratching the clay surface with a modelling tool or comb. Slip is then applied to the scratched surface thereby providing a type of 'clay glue' and the two pieces of clay can be pushed firmly together.

Wedging

Wedging is the term used to describe preparing clay by kneading it, just as a baker would with dough when making bread. A wooden surface is usually available in a room where clay therapy is being offered and this offers a good platform to work on. I have often seen children move naturally into kneading clay in therapy sessions whilst telling me they are making bread or pizzas.

Thumb Pots & Pinch Pots

When holding a lump of clay in our hands we seem to have an instinct that urges us to push the thumbs and fingers into it or to pinch it into a shape that forms a container. Early humans did this and so, too, do young children. By rolling, patting and slapping a lump of clay in the hands we notice that this is probably the simplest way of shaping a sphere or ball.

It takes effort and energy to mould clay and so when a recognisable shape appears the maker experiences a sense of achievement — wonderful for building self-confidence and

Construction Techniques — front to back — coiling, thumb pots, (pinching technique) and slab work technique.

self-esteem! I always aim to have lumps of clay available in a variety of 'hand sizes'; that way clients can choose if they desire a small manageable cube, or a big chunky piece that will provide a challenge to the thumb pot maker!

A helpful way to begin shaping a thumb pot is to cup the clay in one hand, whilst pushing the thumb of the other hand gently into the clay. I suggest the maker gradually pushes down towards the —dening the shape with a circular movement of the thumb. Thumb pots are usually restricted to hand-sized models. Pinch pots are simply variations on the theme, in which greater use is made of 'pinching' the material into shape with your fingers.

Other than this, I offer few suggestions. This is a therapeutic use of clay and the aim of therapy is to enable the client's personal exploration and experimentation, discovering their own resource-fulness and ability to make decisions in the process.

Coil-Building

Throughout the world the technique of coiling is still used to make decorative and functional pots. It is one of the oldest methods of pot construction, although it does require a little practice to be able to make reasonably shaped coils.

When we work with children in clay therapy we notice that it seems perfectly natural for them to roll clay in the palm of their hands to make sausage shapes, but that they progress on their own towards creating tall constructions with the sausages. On the odd occasion we will see children venture into making coil baskets, but these are of a low height, though this is dependent on a child's level of manual dexterity. More often than not young children will use simple coils to make food and meals or even benches or huts.

Interestingly some adolescents are a little more adventurous and want to explore and push the clay (and themselves) to see what can be made and achieved. What usually happens is the older primary school child or adolescent will work at building coil (sausage) upon coil (sausage) because they may have been taught this in pottery lessons in an art club or at school.

The therapist who feels no need to hurry or rescue the young client is providing a nurturing environment and secure space for experimentation. The waiting and observing with interest what is gradually unfolding is such an enabling time. Some clients like to begin with a slab of clay (see below for slab making) cut to form a base on which to build the coils and others like to curl long coils round to make a sitting snake shape. Everyone finds their own preferred way of working with coils.

I tend to take a lump of clay and begin by gently squeezing until it is more of a sausage shape. If the clay sausage becomes too long to manage, I break a part off so that I am working with a manageable size. Next I put the sausage on a wooden board and, placing my two palms together downwards over the clay, I gently start to roll it out from the centre. I let my hands travel outwards with the clay as the coils get longer. Usually I will keep my fingers close together rather than spread wide as my palms do the rolling throughout this process, as I find it gives me more control over the clay as the clay stretches, but I often notice small children becoming quite excited when the ends of the sausage begin to jump around on the wooden board. Giggling accompanies this, as does much eye contact, so coiling can be good for building relationships and working on attachment issues with clients!

Do monitor the dampness of clay while working with the coiling technique, since over-working the same lump of clay will dry it out and lead to shapes and forms that crack. A dampened cloth can cover the clay and keep it moist when it is not being worked on.

Tiles & Plaques

Children and adolescents frequently make tiles or plaques in clay almost as if they are making a flat, horizontal pattern or picture. This technique is easily tackled by most age groups. The idea is to make a flattish sheet of clay, either by patting or flattening with the palms of the hands or by rolling out the clay with a wooden rolling pin. If an even thickness of clay is desired, then it helps to place the clay between two wooden slats of the same thickness and roll it. Remember to carry this procedure out on a wooden board as the clay will stick to a Formica surface, causing difficulties when trying to lift and move the tile or plaque. What is lovely about this technique is that the sheet of clay can simply be left in the flattened shape with rough or organic edges, or made more geometric with the help of a pointed tool to cut the edges more uniformly.

Scratching or etching onto the tile or plaque surface provides decoration as well, allowing the possibility of adding names and dates to the clay. Alternatively, additional smaller sheets of clay may be added to the base plaque as relief detail, whilst grasses, leaves and natural materials can also be pressed into the clay. For example, a base cloud shape can be cut from the sheet of clay and zigzag lightening shapes, or sun shapes added. Fingers are often pushed into the clay to make impressions. An example of this might be a small island base where the fingers have been used to press down the edges of the clay to look like waves or rock pools.

Slab Building

The slab building technique is a versatile method for constructing models of some height, thus offering a real creative exploration. Using the method described above for rolling out an even slab of clay between two wooden slats of the same thickness, it is possible to create rooms, buildings, gravestones, or containers, if the slab of clay can be wrapped round a core support. The secret of the slab-building technique is to know that soft clay is better for wrapping round supports and slightly harder clay or leather-hard clay is more conducive to making buildings since firmer clay will stand erect better than soft clay.

In therapy sessions young people usually want to get on with a creation, not affording time for the clay to harden. However, it is worth remembering that the work in a therapy session is generally transient and more about the process rather than creating aesthetically pleasing and beautiful models. Another helpful tip when building up slabs of clay is to ensure that all joins inside a slab construction are as strong as possible, especially if the client intends to keep the work. Strength is gained by scoring and adding slip to the edges about to be joined and then smoothing over the join with a tool, finger or thumb (see above, 'Basic Techniques').

Sculpting

Sculpting is a technique associated with carving, chiselling or making indentations to create a form in clay. Children are very spontaneous on the whole at shaping and sculpting three-dimensional models in clay. By pushing, patting and squeezing a lump of clay, a shell, fish or monster-type creature might emerge as a sculpt, with decoration being added through carving details or inlaying different coloured pieces of clay for eyes.

Modelling

Modelling in clay is the making of a small scale representation of something or someone the client knows or has seen or imagined. For example, a miniature garden or a plate of food or a friend might be modelled. The modelling is a way of working in clay that most clients are able to do, even when fingers or thumbs are missing.

Client concentration is often something a therapist comments on in supervision. It is surprising how many clients who have been given the label of ADHD, are able to fully focus on modelling in clay for a full session. Sometimes clients have very clear ideas of what they want to make, whilst at other times the model-making is a gradual activity during which the initial idea or construct suddenly morphs into something very different. It may seem quite a basic concept, but it is nevertheless helpful to remember that the modelling of a transitional object or phenomena is itself, quite literally, a work in transition.

Clay models are often made by creating spheres or sausage-like coils from clay. There are few rules apart from ensuring the clay is malleable for bending and folding clay shapes. However, the making of very thin and or long shapes (such as cat whiskers) increases the likelihood of breakages, since thin clay shapes become fragile and brittle when dry.

Modelling the Human Figure: Proportions in Sculpture

The human form can be short and broad, or tall and slim — and something in between. From ancient times artists and sculptors have tried to arrive at the ideal proportions for an aesthetic body shape. The early Greeks and Romans took the head as a unit of measurement and this concept was used to divide the body into eight equal parts. The diagram below gives the general idea.

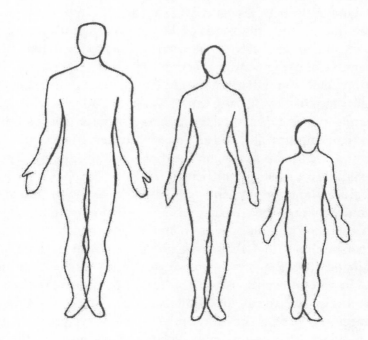

Human Proportions

Notice that a child's proportions are divided into six head units. As a general rule the seven and a half heads size is the mostly used today although the units for male and female shapes are different.

The guidelines are worth following to help with remembering basic proportions:

- Shoulders are two head widths.
- Arms are three head lengths.
- Arms are half width of the head.
- The waist is a little wider than the head.
- The waist appears to be two head lengths from the chin.
- A hand is the same size of the facial plain.

When making human figures, it is easiest to begin by making a sphere for the head as this can be a guide for how big or small the torso should be. Clay coils and sausages help to make arms and leg shapes; and, if the ends of these coils are gently squeezed between a finger and thumb, they can be used to form hands and feet capable of being bent in specific directions.

Young children will often mould simple human forms out of a single piece of clay, giving importance to heads, facial details, the hands and feet. It can be frustrating to try to model a figure that is standing upright, so the therapist might suggest that the client makes a seated figure, or one that is leaning against a prop (for example a tree stump or bench).

Children and adolescents generally have lively imaginations and will take the subject of their modelling from the world around them. Their models often show amazing characteristics and personality traits that have obviously been studied and assimilated into the mind, but are probably not consciously available for discussion until a clay person materialises. Interestingly, the recall of detail can be a powerful process and discussions of expression and mood offer a great deal of information with broader knowledge and meaning unfolding through the narrative.

Chapter 4

Working with Clay: Creations and Processes

Many therapists who are enthusiastic about working creatively with different mediums but there may be a certain hesitancy when deciding how to help a client explore the created image or process. This chapter will focus on developing further confidence in working with clients using clay and look at four techniques for exploring a client's clay creations and/or processes:

1 'Storying' is the discovery of the spoken story emerging from the clay form or process.)
2 'Titling and metaphor' involves inviting the client to think of a title for the image or process, thus providing the opportunity to observe metaphors that become apparent as a result of the titling.
3 'Personifying' is playful personification of the model or image in clay.
4 'Symbolism' involves discovering personal symbolic meaning within the model or image.

'Storying'

Some clients are very quiet when beginning to work with clay and this is not unusual. In the midst of the quietness so much is happening, and the silence presents an ideal opportunity for the therapist to give the client's process and creation their full attention. This tracking and witnessing conveys to the client that we are following the story of their work in progress. We may nod, smile, grimace or tilt our heads to see what could be happening from other angles. All of these small movements are consciously or unconsciously registered by the client. The message received by the client is that what they are doing is worthy of the absolute attention by another person. We 'hear' the client's story through the process unfolding in front of us. Therefore, all the senses must be alert when working with clay.

Witnessing the forming of a clay image/process

As the client starts to sculpt with clay in therapy, aim to work initially as a silent witness who tracks and observes what the client is doing. Look at:

- Expressions on the client's face,
- Changes in breathing,
- Physical movements of the whole body, but more particularly what the hands and fingers (or other limbs) are doing with the clay,
- Words or sounds uttered,
- Forms and shapes — representations or images emerging and changing in the clay,
- What the creation looks like from different viewpoints, especially since the therapist will be sitting at a different angle to the client.

When speech accompanies the clay work

Children and adolescents sometimes provide a running commentary on what they are doing with the clay and this can be rewarding for the therapist, since there are natural places to interject or clarify what is happening, thus improving everyone's understanding of the work. This experience is described as 'storying' with the clay; in other words, both the client and the therapist are co-creating and telling the story together. A narrative in this situation really does open up so much potential for new meaning to come to the surface, enabling the therapeutic work to be moved on, sometimes at a fast pace. Imagination and imagery play a large part in the storying process when working with clay and focussing intently on the client's process helps to identify themes of their narrative and to illuminate any unspoken undercurrents in their story. Recording this in the therapy notes after the session offers a resource to be shared in clinical supervision.

Four Avenues of Exploration

However, there are always clients who are reserved or hesitant to talk about the clay process and, of course, language development needs to be considered as does the age of the client. At times like these it helps to work through my 'Four Avenues of Exploration', first formulated in *Touching Clay, Touching What?* (Souter-Anderson, 2010) These avenues do not necessarily follow sequentially, but are offered as a guide to fascilitating 'storying':

- Together the client and therapist consider what has been created: has it been a process or has an identifiable image been created? View the work from various angles (front, back, sides, top and underneath).
- Aim to recall how the process or creation was formed through the physical movements employed when working with the clay.
- Ruminate on the emerging feelings and emotions.
- Consider and appraise what the client thought was significant when talking about the clay process or image.

Titling and Metaphor

Upon hearing the story accompanying the clay creation or process it is helpful to listen with particular attention to the actual words employed, then to pick up specific usage of a certain word or phrase and reflect it back to the client. This helps the client to register the 'storying' process. When the time feels right, which is usually towards the end of the discussion, invite the client to give the creation or process a title. Ask them not to think too hard about this, but to go with the flow because the spontaneous response can be more revealing. Usually, but not always, the client will come up with a title. The title might be one word or several words — and it may well be a conscious or unconscious metaphor for an issue in the client's life.

Metaphors depend upon use of the imagination and are words or phrases that show how the clay creation or process may share certain qualities with something else in the client's life. This is where the mind can throw up a smoke screen, since it is not always realised or appreciated (by client or therapist) what the metaphor implies. Freud likened this to the mind 'talking in riddles', and therefore it is important to adopt a creative approach to exploring what the possible meaning could be. It can be advantageous not to be too literal. For example, the client called his clay animal 'Tommy the tangerine tiger'. This conjures up a picture or essence of what this wonderfully descriptive title metaphor might be. Another metaphor offered by an adolescent client was 'The golden garden'. These metaphors provide a rich mind picture for the therapist and client to work through and with.

Personifying

When the clay creation or process has become recognisable, or if the client is puzzled by what has appeared in the clay work, it may seem appropriate to invite the client to talk to the image. This exercise is easier to understand if the clay image is a person or an animal. For example, you could invite the client to ask the giraffe why his head is so floppy, or to speak to the gargoyle about why he looks so angry. The same method is just as effective when talking to inanimate creations. For example, the car might be asked how it feels about crashing into the mountain. When the client has posed a question or spoken to the clay creation, follow this by asking the client to 'become' the giraffe, the gargoyle or the car and to reply to the original question.

When facilitating this process of personification, the therapist needs to fully concentrate, because the answers are often un-expected. This is a powerful way of working with clay images, so the therapist's awareness that they are functioning in the role of an 'emotional midwife' needs to be at the forefront of their mind. I refer to this stage as 'Lens 4: the bridging process' (see Chapter 1, 'Theoretical Underpinning of Clay Therapy'. And Appendix, 'Theory of Contact: Physical, Emotional, Spiritual and Metaphorical').

Symbolism

It is helpful to remember that symbolic work, according to Jung, is the language of the unconscious and that transformation, change and a move towards feeling more whole can only occur by means of this symbol work. At times the client may imme-diately recognise the clay image they have created, but at other times the client just does not 'see' an identifiable form in the clay. If this is the case: and while doing so the client invariably recognises a known image.

When this happens the work begins to move into some personal symbolic meaning; that is to say what has been created is perceived as standing for something else, through association of ideas. It is important not to rush or push symbolic understanding upon the client. Rather, the symbolic meaning will unfold as and when the moment is right for the client. Significantly, the clay forms that come to be recognised by the client aid in directing the psychic energy to a previous time when emotional development had been halted in childhood, for various reasons.

A symbol cannot consciously and intentionally be made from clay. The clay creation that is recognised as a symbol appears when a client is limited or trapped by current modes of behaviour that are inadequate to meet the presenting worries or crises. The personal psyche is quite extraordinary in knowing where reparative work is needed. As the clay image is worked. new meaning begins to permeate a client's conscious awareness, bringing with it the potential to enhance life through a process of thought reconfiguration.

Long after the clay image has been made and symbolic expression has been understood, the visible form may still be pregnant with meaning and potential, suggesting that the clay creation still has energy and is alive with significance. When working with clay, something within the client is metaphorically touched and, having been touched, attempts to reveal itself, to make itself known. Put simply then, the clay acts as a bridge between the outer and inner worlds of the client.

When writing notes after sessions, the therapist may find a dictionary of symbols as a reference source helps to give broader understanding of the personal symbols made by clients. This can be especially useful when presenting case material for discussion in clinical supervision. Here, a deeper exploration of symbolism potentially affords further insight into the work.

Finally, it can be very helpful to photograph clay forms and processes, as pictures of the workings provide a good impetus for clinical discussions, whilst clients themselves, often enjoy having a photographic record of their therapeutic creations.

Chapter 5

Developmental Phenomena with Children and Adolescents in Clay Therapy

Children and adolescents show a wide variety in their physical manipulative skills and resourcefulness in terms of construction. Naturally the physical, emotional and intellectual development of each young person needs to be taken into account when considering what to expect when using clay. Many people who are physically disabled may show real skill in modelling with clay and gain much pleasure in making something recognisable, whilst young people with learning difficulties can display patience and perseverance in their clay work to the extent that the therapist is, at times, required more as a technician than therapist.

The developmental descriptors below are a synthesis of my own experiences, based on my professional training and clinical practice. It became clear in the course of this clinical experience that because communication is a key concept in clay therapy there was a growing need in the profession for recognisable descriptors. In 2012 descriptors were created for children's developmental modelling and sculptural abilities, and these have proved invaluable to therapist since little existed previously in this field.

The descriptors give an idea of what could be considered developmentally appropriate in terms of working and modelling with clay, but it must be remembered that clay work does not always correlate to what may be considered normal artistic development. Rather, the medium of clay can provide insight into the emotional state of the client through observation of their movement and energy, and the opportunity to study their facial expressions. Prior knowledge of a client's special needs and considerations is essential information that should be gathered at assessment meetings with referrers, although occasionally this is not possible. For example, there may have been a change or deterioration in the client's functioning abilities as seen with life-limiting illnesses.

Descriptors for Children's Developmental Modelling & Sculptural Skills with Clay (2012)

The descriptors should only be used as a guide and should not be taken as fixed points of reference.

Up to 2 years

- Until children are around 2 years of age, they tend to *respond* to the clay rather than *work* with it.
- Short attention spans mean there is little sustained effort when touching clay, though usually there is a sense of curiosity, perhaps bemusement. There is certainly frustration at what clay will — or will not — do when patted, poked or prodded, for this is a medium that may remain unchanged unless vigorously worked.
- Pinching can leave a noticeable dent in clay but does require a fair degree of effort from little fingers and often a small child does not have a firm enough pinching ability to make an impression.
- Since there is little prolonged physical effort, recognisable shapes are unlikely to appear.
- The small child is still in the sensorimotor phase of development so there can be a fundamental need to taste the clay, making careful supervision essential.

Around 4 years old

- Attention spans have usually lengthened by the age of 4, but frustration may set in easily when the clay does not respond to the child's wishes.

- Some recognisable shapes begin to form, but these are crude and rough in appearance. Conversely, the desire to experiment and explore the medium without instruction may be noticed at this age.
- Some young children do acquire a sense of achievement when a basic form is made. An example of this can be the making of clay chips or peas.
- 'Pretend play' with clay often extends to a small lump representing a cake or chocolate bar.
- The strength to flatten clay by squashing it with small hands helps this age group to make 'plates' or 'bowls' for food.
- Shape cutters such as moons or stars can be provided to use with clay. However, tight corners in the cutters often mean that when the clay is removed from the cutter the shape is not as the child had hoped, leading to frustration.

Around 6 years old

- Children are likely to work with more sense of purpose as motor skills develop, with repetitive actions making a difference to the creation of forms.
- Sometimes children of this age group will seek assistance in making a specific creation. An added advantage here can be a feeling of relaxation as this occurs, enabling further levels of experimentation.
- Spheres and sausage shapes may be attempted.
- Basic human forms and figures begin to appear, along with the urge to model familiar people, such as family members and pets, particularly as more sophisticated perceptual qualities are exhibited.
- The use of wooden rolling pins and modelling tools helps to give more even, flat shapes, so human and animal faces may begin to appear.

Around 8 years old

- By age eight much progression is seen in terms of manual dexterity as concentration levels increase and absorption in the task can be observed.
- There may be a loss of creativity due to expectation of the same kind of instructions that children experience at school.
- Modelling skills develop as the desire to add easily made detail increases. More developed problem-solving abilities aid further experimentation and achievement: for example, hats, bags, newspapers are made.
- Occasionally results can be unexpectantly successful through trial and error.
- Variation in size and proportion of human forms modelled can emphasise their importance in terms of relationships.
- At this age children usually enjoy talking about their ideas, with their narratives being quite imaginative.

Around 10 years old

- Realism begins to be seen in models, with gender detail becoming significant, whilst cartoon figures are also some times modelled.
- Faces, hair and clothing may also appear.
- However, imaginative play with clay often leads to the use of symbolism and metaphor making in this age group.
- Some children around this age are able to express views and make value judgements about their clay creations and processes.

Around 12 years old

- Modelling and sculpting skills may never move much beyond this development stage of manual dexterity. This happens for many reasons, but mainly because art teaching ceases around this age for many school children.
- For those who do progress, greater detail is seen along with the emergence of some abstract images and concepts.

● Symbolic representation and the use of metaphor can be stronger elements of clay work, as this age group is usually capable of organising thought processes sequentially and logically in communicating experiences and narratives.

If you wish to work with a trained therapist's eye and take these developmental descriptors into account, noting their emotional content in particular, it is possible to have an objective response to clay processes and creations in a therapy session with children without necessarily knowing the client case history. This has been significantly borne out using the case studies in Parts Two and Three and the research theses in Chapter 16. When studying case notes and accompanying photographs of clay images, there was an 88 per cent correlation between the type of clay image, client details and the age group descriptors outlined above.

Broader Phenomena

Mental illness, in children and adolescents whether mild or acute, (for example depression or phobias), renders the loss of self-esteem a major consideration in clay work. If such illnesses are the case, then working on building confidence is imperative. It is surprising how the concentration required in clay therapy is notably beneficial for clients with depression, since the mind is occupied on something other than the troubled mental state. Likewise, the developmental abilities of children and adolescents who have been subjected to traumatic experiences are likely to be arrested at the stage when the trauma took place. This means that the creative link between fingers, hands and psyche will take the client back to the point where their emotional functioning ability was halted in an attempt to offer a repairing facility that could potentially lead to healing. The descriptors for creative abilities at different ages should be remembered when viewing clay creations or processes.

Studying clay creations in therapy sessions suggests that when the client's psyche is 'on the move' the quantity of images accelerates, with one series provoking or triggering the next. That is to say that the more sculpts that appear, the more the 'working through' of client issues is evidenced, with noticeable shifts in the therapeutic work being apparent. It may be safe to suggest when there is a good level of client immersion in the clay work, emotional changes may be noticed. This transmuting process is at the core of symbolic manifestation and metaphorical workings. As a result, serial non-directed clay work with children is usually more beneficial in revealing that which requires 'working upon' psychically rather than are directed clay sessions during which less emotional information surfaces.

Furthermore, the client seems to be making meaning and sense when there is continuous involvement and contact with the clay, suggesting a transformative process is underway. In other words, the client's previously unrefined thoughts are being worked whilst the clay is also being manipulated, giving an opportunity for new understanding to evolve. The actions, noises or narrative that accompany the process all provide extra information to guide the therapist in seeking to understand and reflect meaning on what has been taking place.

Creation of entire scenes in clay can show a greater level of developmental sophistication, as opposed to the making of a single image or figure, as does close attention to detail. This information assists the therapist when considering how the therapeutic work is flowing and can provide enriched, worthwhile discussions in clinical supervision or when written reports are sought. Likewise, the complexity of clay constructions tells of a more developed skills base and knowledge utilisation, thus corresponding to an ability to play with ideas and concepts as thought processes turn into more concrete images in therapy. Whether a young person creates a flat, pictorial, almost two-dimensional sculpt or models, or a three-dimensional form that stands up, seems to be dependent upon the perceived work. For instance, a large tree would be difficult to execute standing up in clay, so the client draws on their problem-solving skills in making a discreet decision to create it in two dimensions. This leads to an appreciation of elaborative narratives where insights may permeate.

Therapists may find it useful to view clay creations in terms of masculine and feminine aspects. If working from a Jungian perspective this would be described as the anima principle when seeing feminine subjects or qualities, whereas the animus would correspond to the masculine subjects or qualities. Further understanding on these principles can be gleaned through careful consideration of case history and case material, thereby offering a broadening and deepening in the quality of the therapeutic work.

Choice of Clay Colour

The unconscious choice when selecting red clay or grey clay is worthy of further research. It still seems too early to hazard a guess at which colours are used when particular issues are being worked with. Any such theory would be too simplistic, as the reasons for use of various colours of clay are likely to be far more complex. The significance of colour choice may, however, best be observed at the point when a client shows disappointment or pleasure at the colour of clay provided. What has been observed, is that grey clay is often selected when working on issues surrounding death, while red clay is often used when notions of nourishment and nurturing such as food, birthing and mothering, enter the work in therapy.

PART TWO

CLAY THERAPY
with Children: Case Studies

Chapter 6

Toileting Troubles:
Evie (age 5)

Reasons for Selecting this Case

Practitioners often express a desire for guidance about what to do when things go wrong in therapy sessions, and so Evie's case has been included to assist practitioners in considering specific aspects of the work and how each individual therapist may choose to respond. Unintentional mistakes are part of the necessary process of failing the client and allowing her to locate her true self.

Introduction

There has been considerable increase over the past ten years in children being referred for therapy whose presenting problem is to do with toileting difficulties. Each time such a case occurs, therapy has revealed a deeper underlying problem, usually undetected by adults in the family.

Case Background Information

Five-year-old Evie was a delightful child who was referred for therapy because the family medical practitioner had intimated the concern could be psychosomatic. He had proposed that Evie may well respond to a therapy intervention before medicalisation of the problem occurred. Such medical practitioners are gems. It is a sad fact that at such a young age, some children are still subjected to intrusive and invasive medical investigations; happily this was not going to be the case for Evie.

Evie lived with two parents; her mother was of Italian decent and her step-father from Scotland. She had a twelve-year-old step-sister, who was described as a youngster destined to be a high achiever and a nine-year-old autistic brother who required specific attention. He was her biological brother.

Therapeutic Work

I had been warned in the assessment session with Evie's mother that her daughter could be 'quite a handful', so I was wondering what to expect. In fact Evie could be heard before she was seen! Somewhat loudly, almost to announce her arrival, she was heard in the corridor singing a well- known, children's song:

> Miss Polly had a dolly who was sick, sick, sick,
> So she called for the doctor to come quick, quick, quick.
> The doctor came with his hat and his bag
> And he knocked at the door with a rat-a-tat-tat.
>
> (Anonymous)

Evie's mother made to introduce her to me, but immediately Evie started up the song again. My natural reaction was to join in with Evie's singing and she seemed to welcome this. Evie's mother, somewhat flustered, said she would return at the pre-arranged time and I nodded. Still singing, Evie stepped into my room, looked around and this time shyly sang the song again, whilst waving a hand-knitted doll in front of me so I could not miss it. There is a second verse to this song, but since Evie had not attempted to sing it neither did I. Crouching down and staying with the metaphor of the song, I said, 'Hello Evie, I'm Lynne. I wonder what the matter is with Miss Polly's dolly?'

Sessions normally open with a welcome and words along the lines of: 'When we work together, I make sure you are safe, the room stays safe and I stay safe.' This is followed by a few short sentences communicating my need to tell another adult if I discover, during our time together, that the child has been hurt when she is away from the sessions, but reassuring the child that nothing that happens in our work together is shared outside the room, without the child's knowledge.

With Evie this formality had to wait until the end of our first session, because we were straight into the work. Evie clearly was ready and no time was wasted.

'Dolly has a tummy ache!'

'Oh dear, that's horrible for dolly. Can you show me where dolly hurts Evie?'

'Everywhere. Up here, up here and up here,' she replies pointing roughly in the direction of the doll's stomach.

'Everywhere then; really everywhere?' I sympathised.

Evie likes this and becomes louder and more excitable whilst she twizzled on the spot, waving the doll frantically now.

'Yes, just everywhere, everywhere, here and here and here!'

'Oh dear, what shall we do?' I ask.

Evie is almost skipping round the room now.

'She needs a poo!'

'She needs a poo. Where is dolly going to do her poo?. I reflected back at her.

At this point the doll was flung across the room, as Evie demanded that I make a toilet seat. Fortunately, my creativity was to the fore: I grabbed a towel usually used for hand wiping and twisted it lengthwise to keep it tight before setting on a cushion in a small circle to represent a toilet seat.

'There, we have a toilet for dolly,' I announced.

Giggling, Evie crouched and pushed the doll into the centre of the circle of twisted towel. Once the doll was in place, Evie now took her time making the noises heard when someone is constipated:

'Push, push again, push, push harder. I pooed.' She grunted. During this episode, Evie had instructed me to sit on the floor beside her, telling me that I was sitting outside the bathroom.

'I'm quite pooped!' I say.

Evie thought this hilarious. I followed by asking if the tummy-ache had gone yet.

'Not sure,' was the response.

Given that Evie was a young child, the sessions had been set at 40 minutes duration and, unsurprisingly, the first session was already over.

It is always interesting to see how a new client enters the work of therapy, how they handle the beginning of the first session. Counsellor and therapist training always places great significance on this first meeting and greeting process, and it pays to be vigilant getting the mood and timing just right.

Evie's arrival, heralded by the loud singing of a small child's rhyme, had made me smiled to myself. The sounds from the corridor made me curious as to what I should expect in the therapeutic work we were commencing. And, rightly or wrongly, I formed an opinion about Evie before I saw her: she sounded an energetic, lovely little soul. Indeed, she presented as a charming little girl with an abundance of dark hair that was caught up at each side of her face by little rabbit hair-clips.

Our eyes met; I sensed an immediate connection, an interest in each other. I gathered there was a good attachment style with her mother and that here was a bright and inquisitive child. She scanned me then stated forthrightly, 'You have lots of freckles.' 'Yes, I do.' Wondering where this was leading, but did not need to wait long before I realised the positive transference from Evie had sprung up immediately in our first meeting. 'My Nonna has freckles.' Nonna is an affectionate Italian word for grandmother, and it seemed possible that Evie was intimating I reminded her of her grandmother whom she appeared to like. Here, then, was the potential to work through and with positive transference.

I was looking forward to seeing Evie for the second session, but was taken aback a little when she began to inform me exactly what we were going to do. Some children do plan sessions ahead of the time, but Evie was possibly the youngest child I had ever met to take this route.

'We're going to bake today. Nonna makes good pie,' she informed me.. Then, almost to herself, 'You will make poo pie.' More loudly, 'You will make good poo pie with me!'

Taking Evie seriously I reflected, 'I'll make good poo pie

with you.'

Her smile was slightly mischievous. My reply had seemed to hit the right note for Evie. Then, as she began to open drawers in the plastic stack that housed the clay equipment she explained:

'Okay, I need the rolling pin ... a dish and a knife.'

'You know what you need for good poo pie making Evie?'

'Of course, poo pie good!'

I was bemused by the clarity of thinking and doing, so simply nodded. She knew what she was doing. When she could not instantly locate the container with the clay in it, I was accused of hiding it. In that moment I felt like a naughty little girl and considered that Evie, by acting out, was probably letting me know how life sometimes could be for her, when her older siblings or parents could not find something at home.

Swiftly then, I had switched from being the fondly referred-to Nonna and had been catapulted into the role of a naughty little girl! And I needed to check the naughty responses that were welling up from the imp inside me! Instead, I apologised saying I had not meant to make the clay container hard to find. Evie gave a grandmotherly smile and looked down into my face: 'That's okay. I won't be cross with you today!'

Now I was getting a little lost in the work but understood something significant had just occurred. Was Evie letting me know people get cross with her quickly, I wondered?

Taking a big piece of clay that was really too large for a 5-year-old's hands, Evie attempted to roll it out, announcing she was making pastry. But the task in hand required so much energy which Evie did not appear to have. I was therefore not surprised when she threw down the rolling pin and started squashing the clay with both hands pressed on top of each other. I wondered if Evie was an impatient child, but then decided she was typical of a young child who wants immediate results.

As Evie squashed the clay, I quietly reflected her grunts. She responded well to this, I think, hearing my grunts as encouragement with the squashing process. When she tired of the quashing activity, I was instructed to take over. When exerting effort there are usually accompanying sounds, so as I pushed the clay I continued with the grunting noises. Evie became delighted as my effort and sounds became stronger. She threw herself backwards onto the settee letting her legs flip into the air with abandonment.

I relaxed my efforts and sat still on the floor, whilst Evie took to rolling on her back from side to side. There are occasions when one wonders just what is taking place in the therapeutic work and this was one of those occasions! Evie laughed and laughed as she rocked herself like an excited toddler. Meanwhile I mused that perhaps Evie had missed out on some freedom when younger; perhaps such silliness had been greeted with disapproval in her family?

During the active giggling time I was also aware of how the movement of the diaphragm may allow emotions that have been previously pushed down and held back, to rise, to be released — perhaps to be consciously experienced for the first time.

Suddenly I was remonstrated for being a naughty girl again. I needed to pull myself quickly into role, for I had been enjoying the scene so much in this second session. I said I was sorry, but I seemed to have little control for I kept giggling. Each time I giggled, so did Evie. We were both enjoying the spontaneity of the moments together; playing with each other, enjoying each other's presence.

However, I was brought up sharply as Evie crossly announced.

'Now you've done a pee!'

I considered how I might have done a pee, but spied a pot of water that had spilled over the squashed clay pastry when we had been joined together in child's play. Again, I was in the wrong and told her I should behave myself and my mummy would be cross.

Five days after this session Evie's father contacted me, enquiring how the therapy was going. Naturally I was reserved in what could be shared due to confidentiality, but was never-the-less intrigued and enquired if something had triggered his call.

What I heard was fascinating. According to Evie's father, her toileting difficulties seemed considerably alleviated after only two therapy sessions. Sometimes the feedback a therapist offers a parent is beyond the realms of adult seriousness. In order that Evie's father's might understand what I believed had occurred, I mentioned that it was possible Evie had begun to 'act out' any worries she had in our sessions, rather than 'holding on' to 'excrement' in her life. I heard a mellow Scottish voice saying:

'You mean holding on to the crap?'

'You could put it like that,' I replied.

The phone call, whilst a short one, gave the distinct impression that Evie's father had understood the way a 5-year-old's worries might manifest as toileting concerns. I knew then that the therapy with Evie was unlikely to be long-term, for if Evie's father had grasped the situation he would begin exploratory talks with Evie's mother. So often experience proves that as soon as a client or parents 'get it', we are almost certainly moving close to the ending of the therapeutic work.

'Today you vill av chocolate slop,' announced Evie when she had entered the room for session three.

'Okay, I'll have chocolate slop but I'm not sure what it is Evie.' I noticed we were straight into the work again.

'You'll like it,' Evie told me.

'I see, I'll like chocolate slop today.' Oh dear, I thought, wondering what I was letting myself in for.

'Ere goes.'

'Ere goes.' I reflected.

As Evie took the red clay, she 'dolloped' it into a big bowl and poured water over it. Clearly enjoying the mess, she began slopping it around with a wooden mixing spoon as the clay and water slithered round the inside of the bowl. Next, there was an attempt to feed some of the chocolate clay stuff to me.

'Isn't this lovely?' Evie exclaimed.

'Umm, lovely!'

'Everyone likes chocolate slop.' Evie assured me.

'Really?'

Next followed a quietly spoken sentence in Italian, which I did not understand apart from hearing and understanding the word Bambino. I asked Evie to help me understand what she was saying. She said she had told me in Italian that chocolate milk was wonderful for the baby. I nodded my understanding. I had been imagining that the feeding process was likely to move to a close, but suddenly realised I had been wrong. Evie proceeded:

'Nonna Lynne, you must drink the chocolate slop milk because it is spe-c-i-a-l ('special' spoken dramatically!).'

I heard that I had just been addressed as 'grandmother' in Italian and so guessed that what was taking place held special significance. I moved to drink from the big bowl of clay and water but was told:

'No, no, not yet! This is very spe-c-i-a-l chocolate milk. I need sparkly things.'

'You need sparkly things Evie?' I quizzed.

'Si, si, si, I need yellow and purple sparklies.'

I suggested we look in the cupboard amongst the arts equipment where Evie found tubes of yellow and purple glitter. Excitedly, she roughly sprinkled the glitter over the clay and water mixture, then stood back. Obviously not satisfied with what she saw, she sprinkled the remainder of the glitter over the clay and water. Again, she stood back, thought for a moment, then walked to the shelf where the poster paints were. Picking up the red paint Evie struggled to pour out some red paint into the bowl. Now we had something resembling a magic potion.

'Oh that is so spe-c-i-a-l now. Oh, how delicious. Would you like some of the mixture?' I suggested.

Oh dear! I had interjected too soon: my timing was out, the result being that Evie turned crossly to me saying indignantly:

'No, no, this is your medicine!'

'Only for me? Don't you think you'd like some?' I queried.

'Yuk, for me!'

The minute she grimaced I saw my mistake. When making my notes later, I realised that I had become caught up in the belief that the clay mixture was a magic potion, presumably for

Evie. Perhaps it was, but if so it was only on her own timescale.

So I was the one who had to pretend to drink the sparkly clay and paint concoction. I am not sure if it did me the power of good but as I drank it, I pretended how wonderful it was.

Evie stared as I drank. I wondered what on earth I was doing, or indeed, if Evie knew what she was doing. I think the answer to both questions was probably 'no', but the play was important because medicine was being made by one and given to the other. Clearly, there had been a need to stay in the metaphor of the 'chocolate slop' that turned to a glittery concoction. An alchemical process had just taken place.

As the session ended Evie, on her way out of the room, gave me a furtive glance and quickly pretended to drink some of the sparkly medicine. I smiled to myself; as the door closed I hummed the toddler rhyme, 'Miss Polly had a dolly who was sick, sick, sick.'

In previous sessions Evie had stopped to look closely at the baskets of coloured gems and glass shapes of moons and stars that I kept in the room. Sometimes she had picked one or two up, looked at me, then returned the gems to the baskets. It had already occurred to me that our sessions together would not be long-term, and it seemed to me that Evie had a sound attachment pattern. I was fascinated in what would take place next.

Evie confidently walked into session four, selected a few patterned glass gems and began wondering where the clay was kept, almost as if she thought I had been devious in hiding it. Working in quietness, (although not silence, for there was much being communicated that neither of us wished to or could put into words), Evie splayed out the coloured gems.

She studied each of them. My part was to witness and track what appeared to be a ritual with some meaning, although I could not describe what the meaning might be at that point. Next I, too, seemed to be required to study the gems with great concentration. While I did this, Evie set about pushing some coloured gems into the grey clay she had selected from the container. Intrigued, I wondered what might be happening.

I still am no wiser to this day, yet I stayed with the wonder and in awe of the process.

'This is special. This is special,' murmured Evie reverently. Something profound, beyond everyday words was unfolding. I had contemplated responding in metaphor, but our spoken words can, at times, sound clumsy and intrusive, so I remained silent. Everything that transpired had meaning well beyond words. It is this 'felt sense' that so often guides when moving into the realm of the unconscious. The place where therapist and client emotionally and metaphorically meet is very special.

The fifth and final session went beyond all reasoning, for Evie came and did that which felt so extraordinary. She calmly entered the room, greeted me with a warm smile, then moved across to the baskets of the very tiny miniatures. Methodically she started sorting them on the floor into categories, then she stopped when she found a tiny brown plastic baby that was no more than two centimetres in length.

'Ah,' Cooed Evie.

'Ah., I mirrored.

Just then, she stretched across to the clay container, pulled out a small red lump of clay and, cradling the clay in one hand she very gently pushed the tiny brown baby into the centre of the clay.

'Ah.'

'Ah,' I reflected.

I do not remember how many times we 'ah-ed' to each other, looking deeply into each others' eyes. I describe this as a beautiful dance that was quite moving in the moment. The reverie of the tiny brown baby being safely located within the clay felt as if a birthing was about to take place and the going within, in the presence of a caring therapist, could mean a new-ness may emerge. In this fashion, I am reminded of a birthing process that can be experienced in sandplay therapy, when the ego becomes aligned with the Self and a true-ness is experienced at a deeply fundamental level. This was the case for Evie with the tiny brown baby. Evie had returned to the womb for her psychic re-birthing to take place.

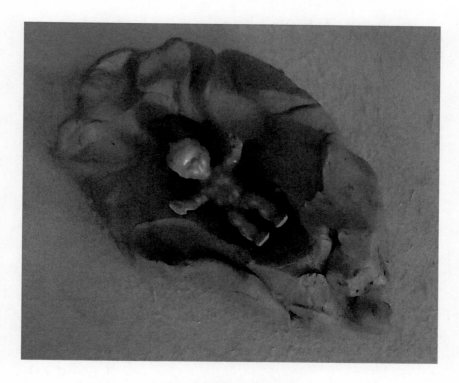

Brown Baby in Clay

I was staggered at the potency of such small actions and activity in this last session with Evie, but her psyche knew what work needed to be undertaken for her to resume a young five-year-old life where toileting issues were no longer a concern for the parents.

Discussion

The therapeutic work with Evie moved at a good pace. My intention in relating the story of her sessions is to illustrate that where the relationship with the client is a good one progress in the sessions can withstand incorrect timing of interjections, and hiccups. Mistakes are part of the necessary process of unintentionally failing the client and allowing her to become herself. After all, it is often when unintentional errors occur that, handled appropriately, shifts in the therapeutic work take the process where it needs to go. Therefore, it is not that we must not make mistakes — it is how we work with them that makes the difference, for we too, are human.

Chapter 7

Parental Separation:
Mattie (age 7)

Reasons for Selecting this Case

This case material aims to illuminate the oft-stated advise in therapy, 'Trust the process.' Until a therapist has experienced this for herself, whether with a client or in personal therapy it appears difficult to comprehend the true meaning. Trusting that therapy 'works' is about trusting in the fact that children and adolescents seem to unconsciously know, almost instinctually, what they need, and will act that need out, whether at home, in school or in the therapy room. Some therapists may describe this process as the psyche's natural instinct to push towards healing; to grow towards wholeness. A young client is usually seeking relief from difficult feelings that they are not always aware of and the use of metaphor often explains to adults that which is elusive for the child to put into everyday language. Logically then, children are angry for a reason, though they need help in locating what it might be linked to.

Introduction

Many 6- and 7-year-old boys present as angry for a period of time and can be hard to see what the cause might be sometimes. It can be enjoyable working with this age group, because identifiable results may be seen within short-term contracts of around 10 to 12 sessions. Essentially, this is one of the age groups in childhood where a growth spurt is seen predominantly in the right hemisphere of the brain and when therapy is able to harness the imagination, thereby intensifying the work in making and using symbols and metaphor.

Case Background Information

Upon meeting both Mattie's parents I heard they were devoted parents to their one and only child. The decision to have only one child was due to both parents following careers in the world of academia. Mattie's father was a university lecturer, his place of work being some distance away from where the family were presently living. He chose to stay at the apartment near his job which the parents had bought when they were working in that particular area before Mattie was born. Due to the father's work schedule, Mattie and his mother often were uncertain which nights of the week he would come home to them. I thus experienced this family as almost a single-parent one, in which Mattie mostly lived with his mother. Ruminating on the possibility of Oedipal issues within the family that might be unresolved, I wondered how much time and attention Mattie would receive from his mother, when he was the only male, albeit a young one in the family home. Did he unconsciously resent his father's expected, though sporadic, re-appearances to claim his established position as the head male within the family?

I gleaned that the parents appreciated and were aesthetes. Mattie's mother was a fine art painter, and his father was a sculptor. With some pride, the parents told how Mattie was good at drawing and painting, winning a local children's art competition the previous year; in their view, this meant he would like working with me through the arts! Apparently, of late, Mattie had become more vocal in not always doing what he was told and his mother spoke of her struggles to discipline Mattie when her husband was away working. Interestingly, Mattie had become quite disagreeable, being outwardly rude to either parent when his father was at home, hence this was the presenting problem for Mattie entering therapy since he was being referred for 'anger management'. I wondered about undercurrents within the family; everything appeared so polite, correct and somewhat genteel, and if this was truly the case I became curious as to what might be angering Mattie. I felt I was missing some vital clue; maybe something was being glossed over.?

Therapeutic Work

The following week I duly met Mattie and instead of a 7-year-old boy. I felt I was meeting a 27-year-old. He presented as so grown up; much too old for his age and overly polite.

'Shall I call you Doctor Souter-Anderson?' he enquired.

'If you wish, Mattie, but in here when we work together we usually use first names.'

'That's good with me Lynne,' Mattie stated.

There was just a touch of precociousness to his manner of speech with a hint of him being on his best behaviour. This matter of presenting a good side through an adopted persona is not in itself unusual, but I felt an immediate pressure that I was uncomfortable about. I considered whether Mattie had been 'straight-jacketed'. Nonetheless I was alert to the probability that there existed an inner tension within Mattie that meant behaving as a well-mannered child was getting too much for him, hence the disagreeable outbursts at home. Probably his polite front was beginning to crack at the edges, for it is a heavy burden when a child carries the family anger.

Mattie ventured rigidly to sit stiffly on the edge of the settee and I could see his discomfort in unfamiliar surroundings; perhaps his experience of free play was limited? I was aware that my opening talk about confidentially and safety contracts for our sessions might be a taste too similar to home conventions on behaviour, so I followed by introducing Mattie to the art materials cupboard, clay storage container and sand trays plus miniatures. He informed me the room was neat and tidy and I instantly thought there would be a real need for messiness in our work together.

When painting at home Mattie told me he always wore one of his father's old shirts to prevent him from getting dirty and that he would bring the shirt in the following week. I accepted this, adding that I had some art aprons in the room that we could use if he wanted. However, I surmised Mattie was attempting to bring in the outside world of home and the familiar. As this was our first session and I was working at building a therapeutic relationship with Mattie. I let the matter be.

'Shall we do some drawing?' Mattie asked in a commanding voice.

'Shall we draw?' I replied.

Mattie followed with, 'Shall I use the white paper?' Then he proceeded to pull an A4 white sheet towards him. He took a pencil, not a coloured crayon although his fingers had hovered over them, and carried out a small drawing in the centre of the paper, telling me he was drawing his dog.

The drawing was a good one for a 7-year-old child; the dog was clearly identifiable and well proportioned. Mattie sat back on the settee, his short legs sticking straight out in front of him and placed both hands neatly together in his lap. Directing his question at me he enquired.

'What shall we do now?'

'We could work in the sand or do some clay or maybe something else?' I responded to his solemnly asked question.

'Some clay?' came the interested rhetorical response.

'Yes, some clay.'

'Umm, some clay!' Almost, as if he was asking himself if doing clay now was acceptable to him.

Next, came the statement: 'We do clay.'

I had just begun to wonder if Mattie was a child whose experience of play was biased towards learning activities. Keeping this in mind, I reached for a big wooden board propped up against the art cupboard and was surprised when Mattie rolled over the large African drum, indicating for me to rest the board on top of it thereby making a tabletop. Then I selected a few modelling tools and some clay talking out loud all the while and describing what I was doing. I ensured each of us both had lumps of clay, because I sensed this young client would benefit from being accompanied in his first attempts to play in therapy.

Throughout my burst of activity Mattie had remained still, simply watching and listening to me. I positioned a small chair towards one end of the drum tabletop, then pulled up a small wooden stool and sat on it. I raised my eyebrows at Mattie as an invitation to join me. He slithered off the settee and sat on the chair opposite.

'What shall we make?' Mattie enquired of me.

'I know,' I responded, 'we'll play with the clay in our hands but not look at what we are doing. That way, it will surprise us when we see what our hands have made. It'll be like a game.'

Mattie pulled a quizzical look. 'Right,' he said.

'Right, okay, are we ready?'

Aiming to turn this into a playful activity. I invited Mattie to make friends with the clay by picking it up, holding it, then letting his hands do to the clay whatever they wanted promising that I would do the same with my clay. Mattie could not resist looking at his clay.

'You're peeping!' I said.

Of course, at that very point I dropped my gaze on to my clay. Mattie found this irresistible and echoed the comment I had just made to him. We chuckled together, and at this point in the working relationship, I had a feeling this was going to be a good therapeutic alliance.

'Okay, okay, neither of us are to peep then, not for a few minutes at least.' I coaxed.

With that I closed my eyes for a couple of seconds as I worked with the clay. Upon opening my eyes, I saw Mattie had his closed as well. A quietness had descended in the room and all that was to be heard was our breathing movements as we worked the clay.

'Are you ready to look at the clay yet, Mattie, to see what your hands have been doing?'

'Maybe,' Mattie softly said.

'Maybe let's carry on a little longer then?' I suggested.

Mattie followed. 'I like this.' I think he was also saying that he liked the quietness, the closeness and the togetherness.

'Yes.' I simply replied.

When it seemed the right time to look at our clay creations, I moved the work forward, suggesting we turn our creations around to view them from different sides in order to see if we could recognise any specific shapes. Mattie did this with his clay and offered he thought he could see a car shape; he showed me where he thought the wheels could be, but then decided it was more of a dinosaur shape. He pointed to where he could see a dinosaur head. We then viewed my clay creation and Mattie got excited pointing out where he could see a bird's nest. I agreed the shape did resemble a nest. I then suggested we could carry on working modelling our clay creations if he wanted to. Mattie was eager, so we talked about what we were doing and what progress we were making as we added detail. In such a short span of time Mattie had dropped his formality showing a playful, creative side to his character.

As we both admired our own and each other's clay models, I talked of what was to happen to our work. because the end of the session was in view. When I had described our creations as 'swell,' Mattie pranced on the spot like a leaping hare. It was apparent Mattie wanted to continue with the dinosaur and nest in the second session, so I showed how to wrap up our work to keep it moist in readiness for the next week. When Mattie's mother arrived to collect him, he left the room. 'We had a swell time,' he told his mother as he leapt along the path.

Mattie arrived for the second session, but the aforementioned painting shirt did not! For this session he was dressed in more relaxed clothing. The initial stiffness of our first meeting was completely gone, as he unceremoniously catapulted himself through the door landing on the settee. Mattie's eyes scanned the room and I guessed he was looking for the clay creation from the previous week. I reached for the airtight box storing our work, which was positioned on a high shelf and, as I turned to face

Mattie, I almost fell over him, for he was so close to me physically.

'Upsey,' I squeaked.

'Upsey,' Mattie imitated. I wondered if I was a bit of a curiosity for Mattie, since he seemed to be picking up on phrases I used.

During the second session the clay dinosaur and nest were respectively worked on and completed. We conversed with each other, but the focus had remained on the work in hand. Mattie decided he wished to leave the clay creations to fully dry out, so I warned him that they would change by the following week, both in colour and size. He nodded his understanding of what this meant.

Later, when writing my reflections on the session, I reminded myself of dinosaurs being symbolically something primal and ancient, and that a nest could be an empty one or one awaiting the birthing of eggs, or one where a parent has flown the coop! I recalled the reason for Mattie's referral to therapy as being 'anger issues'; and as yet I had not seen evidence of that problem, but felt sure some aspect would reveal itself at some point. I did not need to wait long!

Since the first two sessions had been reasonably positive, with Mattie always affable, I think I had let myself be lulled into a false sense of security. I had forgotten my usual caution over never assuming anything in the work. The third session commenced with Mattie bursting through the door, asking for the clay creations. He had obviously forgotten that the clay images would look different in colour and size after a week of drying out. Mattie's look of anticipation changed to one of disappointment and I sensed a wave of disappointment and I sensed a wave of sullenness come into the room.

I commented on the disappointment I had seen on his face. I knew he had heard me, but he chose not to respond. He stared at me with a hint of hostility, and I surmised he did not respond well to change. 'Is this a big disappointment or a little disappointment?' I checked. The response I received was a shrug of the shoulders. When unsure as to what to do next, I do nothing. I did not rescue Mattie, but stayed with the awkwardness that conveyed he had suffered a big disappointment.

Mattie sat down with slumped shoulders, in his usual place on the settee and looked at the floor.

'My Dad isn't coming home this weekend.'

'Not this weekend?' I responded.

'No, he didn't come home last weekend.'

Here was a clue that all perhaps was not well at home, though again I reminded myself not to assume anything.

'Is it unusual for Dad not to come home at weekends?' I gently enquired.

'Um, sort of… sometimes he stays at work in the week, but he always comes home at weekends.'

Mattie seemed upset. His disappointment over the change in the clay creations was beginning to seem as if it might be displaced disappointment in his father's change in week-end homecomings. Mattie's mood slipped into lethargy and disinterest as he asked what time he was being collected and how long it was before the end of the session. I noticed that I had a feeling of foreboding. This was disconcerting, given the good start to the therapeutic work. Sessions like this can be troubling for a therapist, although experience has taught me to sit with the feelings and emotions being presented.

As I held the quietness, I wondered if I was picking up some anger from Mattie, instead I detected the disillusionment Mattie was experiencing, which made him appear sad. It was essential to contain the difficult feelings and emotions within the room, and Mattie feebly attempted to interest himself in other resources available. It was as if he was passing the time of day with me. I packed away the clay dinosaur and nest in their original container and returned it to the shelf. When the session was over I was still feeling the sadness from the work with Mattie, and I had to remind myself not to have expectations for the forthcoming week telling myself, 'It will be as it will be.'

The hint of hostility I had felt from Mattie in session three arrived at the start of the next session too, though Mattie showed more energy. He looked into the container placed on the table and stood still for a few moments. From this I pondered that the clay dinosaur and nest must still be alive with psychic energy for Mattie. In other words, the symbolic meaning still held potential.

'The nest's broken,' Mattie stated as he stared at me.

'It must have just happened.'

'Yes, it's just happened,' came the reply with some inkling of malice in the tone. I waited.

'The dinosaur broke it maybe,' said Mattie in a softer tone.

'Could he have done that?' I queried.

'Yes, dinosaurs are very strong. Have you seen skeletons of them at the London museum, for I have?'

'Many years ago I saw some,' I confirmed.

Now we were moving into a conversation and I knew I needed to listen very carefully for the theme Mattie was actually trying to share.

'The skeletons are ginormous. They were scary animals.'

'Yes, I would have been very frightened if I met a live dinosaur!' I said in an animated way.

At this point Mattie snarled and lunged at me with his hands positioned as claws. He stopped about half a metre away from me. 'Oh, I'm frightened,' I squealed.

Mattie came alive, snarling and lunging at me a second time. I crouched down making myself into a smaller animal. Pretending to defend myself I snarled back with less ferociousness than Mattie had shown. Now he was ready for a fight and we snarled, roared and lunged all around the room in dinosaur mode. A 7-year-old in the role of an angry dinosaur is quite something to keep up with, so my energy in roaring gradually lessened. Mattie must have picked up on this for he surprised me by saying,

'Excuse me Lynne, can we make more clay dinosaurs?'

'That's what you would like to do now? You'd like to make dinosaurs in clay.' I checked.

It is worth noting that throughout this fast action, Mattie never made actual physical contact with me. Should he have done so I would have worked with it, reminding us both about staying safe and not hurting each other.

Given that Mattie had been a physically stiff child when first entering therapy, I thought he had loosened up considerably. The inner tension he had been attempting to suppress had reached bursting point, hence the 'anger issues' at home and the speed at which he became ready to work on that which was desperate to surface. Children are amazing, for they are not as inhibited as adults can be in therapy.

When Mattie moved to get some clay he spotted the collection of standing miniature dinosaurs frequently used in sandplay work. He asked, gazing intently at me, if he could bring them to the place where he liked to work in the room. Selecting three miniature dinosaurs in different colours, Mattie grouped them together on the wooden board where the clay was waiting. He pointed to the dinosaur he made in the first session and confirmed that he had modelled it, but could not remember how he had made it. The atmosphere in the room felt calmer now.

'Yes, you made this one Matti,.' I affirmed.

'Will you help me to make another one?' asked Mattie.

'You would like my help? But I'll need you to be my guide. Will you do that?' I asked, with the intention of empowering Mattie in the session.

'Yes, yes, I will.' He replied enthusiastically.

Our relationship was back on track; a rupture in the therapeutic relationship had been repaired and we were now co-operating. The initial trust from the first two sessions had been tried and tested resulting in a renewed commitment from Mattie. I was expecting to be instructed to make a dinosaur, but instead was told.

'You make a cave for this one.'

'Right, I'll squash out some clay so I can shape the cave, but I'll wait until I know what size the dinosaur will be,' I replied.

Mattie told me to start the cave and not to wait. I understood this as Mattie's wish for me to be working with my clay at the same time as he worked on *his*, making the dinosaur. From the clay-therapy perspective here was Mattie, me and the clay, and out of this something could be co-created, facilitating a new way of seeing, which can lead to a new understanding for the psyche to assimilate. This reminded me of the Winnicottian (1971) notion of playing in the presence of another: in this transitional space between us anything was possible — this was a play space of potential.

Mattie and I were now using the same large wooden board to work on. The three miniature dinosaurs were placed in a standing position to the left of Mattie and his own clay dinosaur sat to the right of him. I had placed myself opposite, although usually preferring to sit at right angles. I pulled the clay container closer to us, and set out some small modelling tools, a rolling pin and a bottle of water close to hand. By now a hush had descended as we worked together, though separately, in our altered states of consciousness. The outside world seemed far away. Nothing else mattered as we worked harmoniously with no words being spoken.

For a 7-year-old, Mattie's observational skills were advanced. When starting to make this new dinosaur, he checked details on the miniature dinosaurs to help him with his modelling. I was impressed and made some accompanying 'mmm …' utterances. Aware of our head movements, it occurred to me that had a video camera been monitoring our progress from above, it would likely have shown us in a kind of absorbed 'courtship dance'.

When reminding Mattie that the session was moving towards our ending time, I noticed he speeded up in order to complete his dinosaur to his satisfaction. I needed to work more quickly too, to finish the cave I was making. I used a couple of wet-wipes to drape over the squashed and uneven sheet of clay and the 'cave' was then complete. The dinosaur looked quite tall for the cave entrance, so Mattie lent over to round off it's back. Then he laid the dinosaur on its side and with real gentleness, he placed it in the cave where he said it could sleep for the week until our next session.

I enquired if Mattie wished to work on these creations the following week. He replied expressing his desire for the clay creations to be left exposed to the air so they could dry out and confirmed that he had remembered they would dry differently. I added that they would be smaller. 'They will be as they will be,' Mattie replied. echoing my words to him in an earlier session. I smiled at Mattie, and we both nodded slightly at each other, almost bowed, in a knowing way.

We had done well. We had worked co-operatively. Upon reflection it seemed both Mattie and I had been eager to ensure completion of our goal today.

In an eager and friendly manner Mattie entered the room for session five. He instantly picked up the three plastic miniature dinosaurs, bundling them into his left hand, whilst reaching for the large wooden board with his right hand. Carrying the gathered resources, he hurriedly crossed the room towards me. It was abundantly clear I was to get the drum base to support the wooden board for making the table he liked to work on. With no hesitation Mattie stood the miniature dinosaurs in exactly the same position as the previous week. Sitting down on a tiny stool next to the drum table, I looked on with curiosity. Mattie regarded the clay dinosaur from session one, plus the previous week's cave and sleeping dinosaur.

'I like this one,' he said, pointing to the sleeping dinosaur.

'You do, you like this one?' I ventured.

'We did it together.'

'We did do it together,' I confirmed.

'This sleeping dinosaur needs a friend.'

'He needs a friend, this sleeping dinosaur does,' I reflected.

'Yes, he does. He's a bit lonely, so we will make his friend together.' Replied Mattie.

'We will.'

No further instructions were forthcoming as we took our clay and started working. When I am unsure as to what is required of me, I tend to be slow in my actions thereby taking the lead from the client. Mattie chose red clay but as the grey clay was closer to me I picked this up ready to use. Ever vigilant, Mattie noted this.

'We've got different coloured clay.'

'So we have Mattie.'

'That's fine,' stated Mattie.

I wondered about this briefly and considered Mattie to be saying that choice and difference were acceptable between us.

Again, Mattie surprised me with his modelling skills. He created a stegosaurus, whilst my tiny dinosaur was not distinguishable as a particular type. However, Mattie took the tiny dinosaur I had been working on and cradled it in the palm of his hand saying, "He's minute." I noted Mattie had referred to the dinosaur as male.

'He does look minute.'

'He needs looking after. He's all on his own.'

'Who will look after him?' I asked, in a somewhat leading manner.

'This dinosaur I've made will be his friend. They will be friends. Everyone needs friends. You've got friends. I've got friends now. You and me have got friends.'

All this was quite revealing. I watched as Mattie put down the tiny dinosaur near to the sleeping dinosaur in the cave.

'I've got new friends. Mummy says that's good.'

I nodded.

Mattie's mother telephoned prior to session seven to inform me that Mattie had stayed with his father for a long weekend. He had returned and in quite an unsettled state of mind, because his father had told Mattie that his parents were now formally separated and not wishing to spend time together. Mattie had taken this information in a matter-of-fact way initially, but his mother had noticed that he behaved differently in her presence. She could not give any further indication of how the 'difference' manifested itself, just that he was not so amiable with her. It was natural to surmise that Mattie might unconsciously be coming to terms with the fact that he was now the victor in his oedipal desire to win his mother from his father. Perhaps he was struggling unconsciously with the guilt of feeling pleasure that he had won the 'battle'.

Some clients struggle to give shape and form to images

when creating in clay, but this never was the case for Mattie. He was a client whose intentionality was nearly always visible, thereby giving flow to the therapeutic work. This was a joy to observe, particularly in the following session.

Mattie began talking about the clay dinosaurs he had made last week, referring to them as if they were all friends. However, he explained there was a problem because they needed someone to look after them. He went on to inform me that I would look after them through the week when he was not with me, but when they finally left my room — when the therapy sessions ended — they would need a mother to take care of them. I was unsure what Mattie meant and it did not seem right to ask for clarification, for he seemed quite convinced that I would understand his meaning. Here was one of those moments when it seemed more desirable to go with the process rather than show my curiosity. I appreciated all would be revealed in the fullness of the work.

During this session Mattie presented in a subdued manner so I enquired if he needed to share anything with me. The response came in an obtuse way. Mattie told me he wanted to make a clay Daddy dinosaur with his son dinosaur. By now Mattie's level of manual dexterity with the clay was good. He was skilled at making the shapes he needed and proceeded to create the Daddy and son dinosaurs in no time at all, and neither did he request my technical assistance.

I was picking up from Mattie that this was the work he needed to do and he needed to do it on his own. I therefore remained quiet throughout the session, although I made it evident that I was watching and tracking progress all the time. I was unsure if I was detecting a sense of sadness from Mattie, but deduced there was more of feeling of determination and resolution, which had been missing previously. This young client knew how his world was unfolding and was showing me he was dealing with it in his own way, making the time in the session his own by engaging fully in his self-directed task.

Session eight saw the continuation of the clay dinosaur-making activities. Mattie made a mother and father dinosaur this

Dinosaur Parent and Child

time, plus two tiny dinosaurs and played at moving them around the surface of the wooden board. They duly visited different places and had several angry interchanges, but when Mattie brought the plastic dinosaur family from the shelves, interactions between the tiny clay dinosaurs and the plastic ones calmed. I wondered what might have been moving through Mattie's mind, for it was clear something was being worked through. Here, potentially, he was working out how to manage changes in his living environment and how he could still be the same Mattie.

Significantly, in the penultimate session Mattie talked about having two different homes and how things had changed between his parents. What apparently still troubled Mattie though, was his need to know what to do and how to be in his two parents' 'homes'. I looked across to the shelves where the plastic dinosaurs were sitting and opened the box in which Mattie's clay dinosaurs were kept. My intention was not really specific, but Mattie took his cue from my movements. He gathered them roughly into a huddle, then started to sort them firstly into sizes, then colours and finally each was given individual consideration as they were positioned on the floor mat that is patterned by squares.

I was reminded of H. G. Wells' writing of *Floor Games* (1911/2004), in which he describes his understanding of why his sons create miniature worlds and the way that transformation can take place during their play. Mattie began to move the dinosaurs around in groups. I was unable to decipher Mattie's discussion between the dinosaurs and himself because his voice was very low, but realised I was not being included in this activity. Again, I was under the impression Mattie was sorting things out in his own way.

This way of playing then seemed to give way, and Mattie looked up to the shelf where the plastic domestic animals were displayed. Standing up, he moved across to the domestic animals and bundled several into his folded arm. Mattie left the clay and plastic dinosaurs with the domestic animals on the floor just where he had been playing with them as the session came to an end. Whilst there had been little verbal communication between Mattie and me, in this session I could see much had been unfolding.

The final session with Mattie was spent in creating another clay dinosaur, who, according to Mattie, was about to become extinct. I listened intently when on the receiving end of a long lecture as to why this was so. Finally I was told that, furthermore, the dinosaurs just could not get on together anymore because they liked to eat different food. The result was they had taken to eating each other. Young children's minds are fascinating! Whilst the logic is sometimes askew, nevertheless the meaning behind the words is enlightening. I nodded my understanding to Mattie and reflected back my acknowledgement of his reasoning. In a loud and important voice Mattie then announced.

'And now, the domestic animals must learn how to behave. They must all take a lesson from the dinosaurs. If they cannot get on with each other they will become extinct because they will eat each other up.'

What more could I say? Mattie had worked through in his mind and in his own way, the difficulties he had faced during his parents' separation. He made the decision to take all the clay dinosaurs home in a box he had brought to the last session especially for this purpose, and together we wrapped the dinosaurs in soft tissue paper and rested them carefully in the box. This was a rich ritual, affording the opportunity to enter into a remembering process, reminding each other of the story of the dinosaurs.

It was a deeply felt and lovely ending from my perspective. My last words to Mattie were to let him know how much I had enjoyed working with him. I watched a little chap give a backwards, energetic wave with one arm whilst his other arm had securely latched itself round the box. One month later I heard from Mattie's mother that he was much more settled and the dinosaurs had a definite home on his bedroom windowsill. The therapeutic contract had come to an end, and I was left feeling wiser for the experience of Mattie's use of metaphor and humbled that his young psyche was capable of finding a passage through a painful journey.

Discussion

Reflecting on this case I could see how that the child, who has a reasonably stable and settled upbringing with an emotionally available mother, comes to therapy with an inner ego strength that offers a good platform to build on. Mattie was such a child. His world had wobbled, but there had been enough of a secure home life to help him through his parents' separation.

This case material had been introduced to illuminate the concept of 'trusting the process'. Hopefully, the therapeutic journey with Mattie, helps clarify this principle, for it is a discreet and difficult notion to describe.

Chapter 8

Travelling Family Issues:
Danielle (8 years)

Reasons for Selecting this Case

There are many reasons behind choosing to include this case. Perhaps the main reason is to illustrate how a therapist's counter-transference may aid the work or get in the way. It is difficult to believe that therapy happens without counter-transference being around in some form or other, and that is why there needs to be vigilance as to its presence. In the case of Danielle, I believe my counter-transference helped to provide a deep bond between us from the very early stages of the therapeutic work.

The second reason for desiring to write about the work with Danielle is to show how our cultural roots; our ethnicity, are deeply emotional and complex phenomena requiring respect and authentic consideration, and that an honouring of these intrinsic components is essential when working with difference. If working in a natural manner with full awareness, tacit acceptance of difference may be helpful, although some therapists believe that issues of difference should always be overtly referred to.

Self-esteem is a phrase banded around by professionals and parents alike. It is hard to give a specific definition. Here what is meant by self-esteem is a person's own viewpoint or judgement on their value within a family, peer group or social situation. In other words, a self-perspective on whether they see themselves as having 'worth' — of being worthy. Feeling different can have a negative impact on a person's self-worth, or self-esteem, and there is also the accompanying emotional pain of not belonging or being included. This may push people into feeling depressed, anxious and often angry.

A child from a traveller background finds themselves continually in a different stream of our society, and traveller children struggling emotionally are rarely able to access therapy. Traveller children can be subjected to prejudices; obviously professionals endeavour to neutralise this, but it would be naive to think it didn't happen.

Introduction

Primary-school children from traveller backgrounds are generally good attendees at school; However, around the age of 8 children begin to notice differences and comment on them, asking searching questions of each other and adults. Girls as young as 8 may get embroiled in friendship squabbles, which can be upsetting and fraught leaving them feeling rejected and betrayed. It is so painful being left out or unwanted.

Danielle's withdrawn position apparently had led peers to forget about her and she was left out of activities as a result.

Case Background Information

Home is where one starts from. As we grow older
The world becomes stranger, the pattern more complicated
Of dead and living.

T. S. Eliot, *Four Quartets*, 'East Coker' (1944)

T. S. Eliot's lines are an appropriate focus point for the therapist working with children and adolescents when first meeting with their parent, carers or the family.

I worked with Danielle, an 8-year-old girl from a travelling background, whose mother had worked hard to establish a well decorated permanent home. According to information passed to me from Danielle's school liaison officer (the referrer), Danielle's home life was reported to be good, although there was a tendency to sibling squabbling, which, is quite normal in many families. Danielle had an older brother and twin sisters aged 2. In school

Danielle was unresponsive to peers' initiatives to include her in playground games. Her class teacher was concerned for Danielle due to her blank expression where little emotion was expressed.

In a preliminary meeting with Danielle's mother she freely shared family background information, suggesting that this was not a pathological emotional case, and that long term-work was likely to be unnecessary. A short-term contract spanning one school term was therefore agreed upon. Towards the end of the meeting, I met Danielle. She presented as a shy little girl at first, but one who showed a lively curiosity in both me and the room. She studied me with what felt like close, searching attention — I was being weighed up. In those early moments I suspected I would later be challenged and would need to maintain good boundaries (as ever) in our work.

Therapeutic Work

As session one commenced, the shyness I had first noticed about Danielle evaporated quickly when she spotted containers of kitchen and home making toys. These buckets were tipped up with a loud clattering noise. We laughed together. The toys were then left in a heap on the floor. Danielle next rummaged through the art resources shelves and took down different coloured pots of Play-Doh.

She busily made food with the Play-Doh at the low table in the room and purposefully she selected two small toy plates on which to put the food. She made two of everything and offered one plateful of Play Doh food for me to 'eat', whilst she consumed the other noisily. I mirrored Danielle noisily munching whilst we giggled together. Reflecting on this work later I reminded myself how important themes of nourishing and nurturing are in our therapy work with children. The therapeutic work seemed to have started well.

In subsequent sessions more mealtime activities got underway which then gave way to a specific BBQ frenzy during which the large lion and monkey puppet had an altercation. We met for four sessions before the mid-term holiday and in the fifth session, after having had a fortnight break, Danielle came into the room in a much more buoyant mood. Breaks in therapeutic work provide an opportunity to reflect and assess how the therapeutic work is proceeding, mindful that the client's way of presenting may show as regression, stagnation or a leap forward. In Danielle's case I could detect a forward movement emotionally. Boldly, with hands on hips and facing me squarely, almost confrontationally, Danielle told me she did not want to use Play-Doh anymore as that was for nursery children.

'Okay, I wonder what you'll use today then,' I enquired of Danielle.

'I want clay today, I want to get messy.' Danielle said, with a glint in her eye.

'Clay and mess today…' I responded.

Hand-sized, cube-shaped lumps of clay are stored in a transparent polythene bag, placed inside a container with a transparent lid. Danielle saw the clay bucket and asked me to cut a slice of red clay for her using a plastic knife. This was hard to do as the body of clay resisted the bendy knife incision. However, I persisted with carrying out Danielle's instructions. She watched my grimaces and exertions intently, until eventually I handed a slab of clay to her. Slapping it between both hands she squashed and squeezed the clay checking every now and then for the thickness. She seemed to know what she was doing. I risked an interjection:

'Shall I cut more slices?'

There had been no need for me to do this. I was being too hasty. I reminded myself to watch and wait to see what would unfold. It was therefore no surprise when I was ignored. I knew then that Danielle needed me to witness and track her activity, sitting quietly, rather than getting in the way by interrupting the process. It is always probable that when the client ignores the therapist's spoken words there is an uncertainty as to where the task is going — interruptions are quite unnecessary, even irritating. Moving to the art shelves, Danielle spent a little while picking up and shaking, then studying the small pots of sparkly shapes and sequins. She selected mauve and pink sequins carefully pressing a good number horizontally into the clay.

'Magic carpet, no ... not big enough, magic rug.' Danielle muttered to herself.

She was obviously delighted with what seemed to be the finished creation.

'Um, magic rug, um.'

It is always great to hear a client spontaneously bring forth a title for the clay creation. But this title was also a metaphor.

'What is the magic rug going to do?' I asked a little off beam.

'It's not doing anything. It's like the one in my auntie's caravan.'

'Ah I see it's a rug that you already know.'

'Yeah.' Danielle scoffed, as if I should have known that.

As Danielle roughly shaped some clay cushions and carried on impressing more sequins and sparkly shapes into the clay, she talked about her visits to the extended family and how, on one occasion, her aunt had invited her to a cousin's fifth birthday where older cousins were also present. I stored this information away in the recesses of my mind, since here Danielle was being shared a time when she had experienced inclusion in female play and birthdays — although I noticed they were relational friendships.

'You like playing with other girls.' I quietly said.

'Yeah.'

Again, she spoke as if I offered something that I should have known to be obvious. I enjoy hearing this attitude, for I see it as a gain in some confidence. If this is the case, then feeling more self-esteem equates to topping up self-worth.

Danielle was appreciating what she had produced in the session, telling me she wanted to keep the magic carpet and cushions in her box where she was to store all things created in our sessions together. I explained about clay shrinking, then changing colour and lightening when all the moisture has evaporated and that maybe the sequins and sparkles might pop out of position. Danielle nodded her acceptance of these technical facts.

'They will look different when you see the clay creations next time,' I told Danielle.

Danielle considered my explanation.

'Okay, I'll stick the sequins back in if they come out.'
I had not attuned to Danielle's way of being immediately, so I knew the following week I would need to be highly focused in my attention to her.

During the next session Danielle was eager to see how the magic rug and cushions had changed. We were both quite pleased with how colourful they looked. Although the sequins had popped out, as I had cautioned, Danielle was cheerful about gluing them back on. Again, I reminded her that although the rug and cushions would now keep their shape as they were bone dry (this stage in the drying process with clay is known as 'greenware' to potters), they nevertheless could break, thereby necessitating careful handling. I could see from the expression on Danielle's face that none of this seemed to matter to her.

I heard my own need to pre-empt disappointment and disillusionment, in my voice, I know this is how we learn so much in life. My own dislike of feeling strongly disappointed and the knowledge of how much energy it takes to pick oneself up and start again made it imperative that I check the emotions rising within me. This was my counter-transference and I would need to keep a tight rein on my desire to protect Danielle from disappointment after this session. I was fussing like a mother hen, when really I should have been registering Danielle's level of resilience.

When reflecting on Danielle. I considered my own experience of so many moves, from birth through to the age of 18. Whilst my parents gave an optimistic perspective on the benefits gained in moving, what I usually experienced was bewilderment when arriving in a new county or country. The feelings of nothingness, then bleakness surfaced as the pain of disappointment. These childhood life experiences of loss and aloneness laid the foundation for acquiring the skills to rebuild and to refocus pretty quickly. I consider it a personal strength to know I can tolerate voids and that my resilience and resourcefulness are never far away. However, the constant moves have left a residue that pushes me towards constantly seeking the phoenix that rises from the ashes. In my note-making from this session with Danielle, I reminded myself of the need to be alert to the fact that the phoenix only arises again after the loss and meaninglessness have been experienced and felt. For children, it is surprising how they usually bounce back from adversity, but this needs to happen at the child's own pace.

When clients know the ending of the therapeutic work is in sight they usually do a fair bit of emotional shifting in that the therapeutic work speeds up. This was also the case with Danielle. She asked me if I liked caravans.

'You're interested in knowing if I like caravans?'

'Yeah, cos my aunty has one, she lives in it.'

'Is this the aunty that you visit — the same aunty who is mum to the girls you visit?'

Danielle seemed pleased I had remembered.

'I used to live in a caravan, but I live in a house now.'

With this she removed the clay bucket lid and reached into the bag for clay. Selecting a grey-coloured lump, she told me she would be making a caravan in the session, but that she needed me to help her. I eagerly engaged with the request; but when this kind of demand occurs, it generally helps to ask the client for instructions as to how the task should be carried out.

After receiving guidance from Danielle, I fashioned a caravan shape, checking constantly that I was making the correct shape saying, 'Like this?', or 'How's this?' or 'Does it need to be different?' Danielle took the clay caravan out of my hands and showed me when and where it needed to change shape. The caravan was obviously meeting with Danielle's approval, as she leant in very close to me, hanging her head right over the caravan, and we worked in this fashion for quite some time.

'It needs a door and windows,' Danielle suddenly said.

'Okay, do you want to take over the next parts, because you'll know where they go on the caravan?' I enquired.

Confidently she again took the caravan from my hands and placed it on the wooden board in front of her. Taking up a modelling tool she roughly drew a door and then window shapes onto the clay van. Whilst she was engaged, I absentmindedly picked up a couple of small clay cut-offs and twiddled them between my finger and thumb. Danielle had noticed, and asked me what I was doing.

'Not sure.'

'You could make something for my caravan.' Danielle suggested.

'I could. Tell me what you would like making.'

'Some gas bottles,' came the reply.

So I set about rounding off two cylindrical shapes.

'We don't have these anymore, we have a boiler that makes our house warm,' continued Danielle.

'Ah that's what the gas bottles are for.' I queried.

'Yeah, some people think travellers — Romanies — don't have things like heating, but they do.'

Here, in Danielle's own time she was referring to misunderstandings and prejudices, experienced due to originating from a travelling background.

Issues of difference require sensitivity and I showed interest in where Danielle was taking the discussion, which veered towards her feeling different in her school. She shared that she thought some children in the class had said she was poor because she lived in a caravan until one year ago. There appeared some confusion due to a boy in the class telling others that his grandparents had a static caravan permanently parked at the coast and he went there on holiday. This lead on to talking about different types of homes around the world and different cultures and how it didn't mean that one was better than the other, it was just different. Looking intently at me she said emphatically, 'I agree.'

By now the clay work had come to a standstill.

Clay Caravan

Taking more clay, Danielle squashed, flattened and then rolled a slab of clay out and placed her caravan in the centre of it. She then positioned the two gas bottles I had made next to the caravan. Now she told me how she was going to make a garden and I was to make a refuse bin; and when I had done that, I was to make some crazy-paving stones so she could fashion a path to the caravan door. When clients make clay models and scenes this is indicative of a cohesive narrative unfolding, which suggests the ego strength is developing. The remainder of the session was spent harmoniously sculpting where we made a garden for the caravan. This was reminding me of times as a primary school child, when we made miniature gardens in biscuit-tin lids. I had loved being a garden-maker with a friend, and here I was doing something so similar. I thought about disclosing this to Danielle, but then wondered, if she need to know? And would my sharing add anything of benefit to the work for Danielle? Recognising this was truly an issue of counter-transference, the decision not to disclose my experience was made. I kept quiet, although determined to enjoy the closeness that we both seemed to be experiencing. It is always hoped that positive therapy experiences are assimilated by the client, so that they are gradually able to use them in everyday life.

The final session seemed to arrive only too soon, but it was a good one. Bursting with enthusiasm and energy, Danielle told me we were going to have a clay party. With this announcement came instructions for me, this time, to make a clay magic rug and I was told firmly,

'You must use lots and lots and lots of lovely things!'

So, I did and what fun I had! Whilst I was busily engaged in my clay work, Danielle set about making a clay bowl for the small silk flowers she gathered from the shelves. She stuck these into the bowl, and then stood back to admire them. Clearly she was satisfied with the result. Next she modelled two small mugs and some clay biscuits. It was my job to decorate the biscuits with patterns. Oh! We did enjoy our clay party. Whoever said therapy should not be fun? It was my absolute delight to see Danielle sparkle in our last session.

Danielle was ready to end individual therapy sessions, but when the school liaison officer mentioned a space could be found for Danielle in a therapeutic group for girls lacking self-confidence, she seemed to like an appropriate idea. I thought Danielle would do well in such an environment and build on her feelings of self-worth.

In the post-therapy meeting with Danielle's mother I heard how Danielle seemed happier in herself. Mother and daughter had clearly been chatting about Danielle's clay activities and all the minutiae of the work had been shared, including the making of the gas bottles.

Discussion

I so adored working with Danielle. In this case I think I can safely say that although I did not always get my timing of interjections correct there was, nevertheless, a strong therapeutic bond between us. Danielle had picked up my willingness to work with her very early in the first session and I think this happened through the laughter we shared when she had tipped the kitchen and home-making toys onto the floor. But I truly believe there was something more fundamental at work here. I, too, had been a child that had travelled because of my father's occupation. I had attended 11 schools and, as a child, knew what it felt like to feel different, to be an outsider, to want so much to be assimilated into a new group of friends. At a deep, unconscious level, Danielle and I 'knew' each other and I think my counter-transference helped me to 'get it' for Danielle, helping to form that special bond, although I had to constantly monitor this complex stream of knowing.

Chapter 9

Kinship fostering:
Bradley, (age 9)

Reasons for Selecting this Case

The focus of this chapter is to show how crucial it is to establish a trusting relationship between the therapist and the client through good eye contact, whilst working with clay. When making eye contact with another, it is worthwhile to remember, however, that too much can be intrusive for some clients, especially if there have been attachment difficulties in early years during the bonding time between a parental figure and small infant. When a sound therapeutic relationship has been created, this affords a fertile foundation for difficult feelings around early relationships to be explored.

A secondary reason for writing about Bradley was to show that given the restrictions of a very short-term contract to work an early disruption in family attachments, it was nevertheless still possible to offer something therapeutic.

Introduction

Children in foster care often display difficulties in attachment styles. They are concerned about where they belong and who wants them. When attending therapy, fostered children are likely to be confused; this confusion is exacerbated by many complex losses. Belief in the fact of their own existence can seem shaky, while feelings of betrayal, rejection and abandonment may surface at any time, given a relevant trigger.

The fear of feeling unwanted or unloved has such a profound abject impact on a child's developing mind that the emotional agony can be too much to bear. The unconscious undercurrent of this pain translates into thought processes such as: 'If I am not loved, I am worthless, I do not matter therefore I do not exist.' This pattern of thinking has been known to tip a young person into a state of emotional breakdown, although mostly, the self-defense mechanisms which arise within the emotionally injured child, will help to prevent this. Instead, the young person grows a hardened exterior that pain penetrates with difficulty, but yet the earlier, intense pain remains frozen within.

In foster care children ask in many varied ways, 'Am I loveable?" And the result of moving to successive foster homes is that there is a continual worry about how long each new move will last.

Case Background Information

The eldest of a family of three children, Bradley had a younger brother and sister. His two siblings were fostered together in one placement, but Bradley was placed in kinship fostering with his maternal grandmother and step-grandfather. His previous contact with his maternal grandmother had been limited, so began the need to form and establish a bond in this new kinship home. There already existed a tenuous bond with the grandmother (although contact had been limited) due to her links with Bradley's mother, but Bradley's step-grandfather was a somewhat unknown relation. There was therefore a need to both strengthen an old bond and establish a new one in the kinship home.

I met the grandparents and heard the step-grandfather had grandchildren of his own and seemed interested in Bradley's welfare. Bradley's grandmother shared her worries over how to answer Bradley's probing questions about his parents. He repeatedly asked why he could not return to live with his mother who was in her mid-twenties, and whether his father really was his true father. And when could he visit him, as he lived elsewhere in the country?

At our initial meeting the grandparents explained that Bradley, as a 9-year-old child, had little to fall back on in terms of solid parenting, because his mother had not been physically available to him and neither had his father been accessible, thereby resulting in attachment difficulties. There was very little other family background information forthcoming, despite efforts on my part to illicit this, which lead me to wonder what issues we might be skirting around. This seemed a sad case of 'How do I know I exist if I am not sure who loves me?

Bradley was referred for therapeutic work by social care services due to his erratic and difficult behaviours in his kinship foster home and at school. When in trouble, he apparently could not be reasoned with. I was concerned about how Bradley, might respond to a short contract of 12 sessions delivered over two school half-terms since his early attachments had been haphazard and disrupted. Short contracts can bring difficulties, but in this case the funding was extremely limited and it seemed better to offer something therapeutic, rather than nothing.

Therapeutic Work

Bradley presented as a lovely though nervous child in our first meeting, bit I was concerned to know how he would respond to the fact that our work together could only last for 12 sessions. I was aware of the importance of using a promising tone when I relayed this information, rather than pessimistically telling Bradley that we 'only' had 12 sessions. The short-term nature of the contract needed to be presented in a positive light.

After learning of the difficulties in the family dynamics, I also realised the end of our contract should not be compromised in any way and fortunately I never needed to rearrange a session through ill health or for any other reason. This meant that for planned sessions I was consistently available *physically*, although (since I am human) the *quality* of my presence was undoubtedly changed over the sessions!

I considered puppet work might be a suitable modality to

commence the therapeutic work because of the underlying attachment and relationship difficulties, although all the other usual creative resources would be on view in the room. However, Bradley had little energy. He was listless and nervy when using his voice which made puppet work ineffective in engaging him. He did not show interest in the sand tray, running his hand through the sand leaving trails with his finger-tips. This seemed a positive start. He tentatively looked up at me. We exchanged small smiles — a token 'okayness', — no words, just gentle encouragement through facial expression.

Next Bradley put his left hand into the sand, palm down. He repeated this action several times in the left section of the tray. He then stood, dusting sand off his hands whilst turning to look at the shelves of sandplay miniatures. I recall thinking at the time, that Bradley had 'left his mark': he had left an impression of part of himself in the sand for us both to see. Just as the session was coming to an end Bradley gave a swift last look round the room and asked whether he was allowed to use clay in the next session. This had felt like a slow session, a long one. The lack of energy and drive had been infectious, for I was left feeling quite listless and lacking enthusiasm.

Upon entering the therapy room for the second session, Bradley moved across to the sand tray and using only one finger, he briefly made some light patterns in the sand. He then saw the basket of dried sticks, wood and fir cones. He took a stick some 2cms in diameter and drew deeper lines in the sand in straight rows. I think my expression must have been puzzled, because I was aware of Bradley studying me hard. I felt concern also that the expression had been disapproving — or even intrusive.

Both of us paused in uncertainty as a quietness settled between us. I held the silence, pregnant with potential, and waited. Much communication seemed to be taking place through eye contact alone, although at the time I was not able to say what was being communicated. However, what then unfolded assured me it had been appropriate to hold this silence.

Bradley next crossed the room to where the clay boards

lent against the stacking drawer container that housed the clay equipment. Taking hold of a wooden board, he placed it on the low table and put two lumps of clay down on it. Bradley picked up one of the clay lumps and attempted to push the stick into the clay. The clay resisted his gentle movement, so he moved closer to the board, retracted the stick and with slightly more effort pushed the stick in again. Still not satisfied, he stood up, and with much more energy he pushed the stick deep into clay. We gazed at each other and nodded energetically, thinking that he might be checking my reaction to his aggressive action. He took a step back from the board, dropped his arms, let his hands swing either side of him with an air of triumph.

'How's that then Bradley?'

'Yeah' he nodded with mild enthusiasm.

Then almost frenziedly, he began to stab the lump of clay with the stick. Squashing the clay down with the palm of his hand he continued his stabbing actions, occasionally picking up different sized sticks to vary the size of the holes he was making.

For a child who presented as nervous at our first meeting, this energetic, aggressive action so early in the work was surprising. That said, perhaps knowing we only had 12 sessions signalled to Bradley the need to use the sessions profitably; he realised he literally must 'get stuck into the work' by stabbing the sticks purposefully into the clay.

By now the clay was quite flattened and firmly stuck to the board, resembling a badly pot-holed road. However, this was only a beginning for Bradley; he appeared already to be pondering what to do with his potholed creation. Next he used the spatula to scrape clay up from the board, bashed the messy substance a bit and flattened the squashed piece, thereby producing an uneven slab about 2cms thick.

'Something else is going to happen.' I stated.

Bradley nodded, commenting that he had an idea he wanted to model Granddad's allotment.

'An allotment,' I reflected.

'Yeah I go there sometimes.'

I felt inquisitive, I nevertheless quietened my urge to ask questions as it seemed something significant was being worked on. Observing and tracking Bradley's movements and actions, I noticed he began making grooves in the slab of clay with a small stick, a little in the way he had trailed the stick through the sand earlier in the session. He made a number of rows, resembling troughs and furrows, and told me what he was "planting". This included cabbages and carrots, but how the soil on his slab of clay was not always going to be good for some vegetables such as, beetroot.

'But my gran likes sweetcorn, so I must make sweetcorn grow in my allotment.' Bradley said.

The end of the session was fast approaching, but sensing the work was unfolding at quite a pace I mentioned to Bradley we could continue next week with the clay allotment. Bradley was in no hurry to stop working with the clay, so I explained that we could wrap the allotment carefully in a plastic bag and place it in an air-tight container, which meant it would be ready to work with if Bradley wanted to do come back to it later.

In writing my notes up after the session I could see the process of Bradley's work was about something being planted. He was investing in nature and nourishment and that linked with his grandparents. Perhaps he had seen 'future goodness' in the clay work, while at the same time checking me out for 'trust-worthiness'?.

Mindful in session three that my enthusiasm for carrying on with the allotment should not influence Bradley's process, I held back initially from placing the clay model started last week on the clay board. However, I need not have worried because Bradley came boldly into the session asking where the allotment was, and then proceeded to tell me what he was going to do with it next. It is amazing when young clients come to sessions with a plan of what they need or want to do. There is real evidence here that children do think about the therapeutic work between therapy sessions, just as adult clients do. This informs us that work carried out in therapy sessions is important enough to warrant 'mind space' during the child's or adolescent's week.

Bradley looked me straight in the eye, confident that what he was about to tell me was both true and important. For five minutes he educated me on planting seeds in pots.

'Keep them in the dark for several days, check on them regularly and when a small green leaf appears that is the time to bring new tiny plants into the light.'

He told me that the young plants were then kept in his granddad's greenhouse after they had germinated and, when the time was right, he would be helping granddad take the new plants to the allotment. Together, using the tools kept in the allotment shed, they would put the little plants into the ground.

I find the gravity in which such knowledge is conveyed by a young client quite magnificent. I was spellbound. Listening carefully, I summed up my reflection with something along the following lines:

'Bradley you know what you're talking about when growing plants from seeds, don't you?'

'I do,' He replied with a pride which told me his self-esteem was increasing.

I responded with a reflected grunt, letting him know I heard his affirmation of himself. Then I gave him a broad smile and nod and asked him if he had already been to the allotment and shed.

'Oh yes I go with Granddad to help 'cos I'm going to be a gardener when I am older and I am going to grow vegetables for Gran and Granddad when Granddad is too old to do the digging.'

Something good was growing, reminding me that attachment work happens when the conditions are right. In this case Bradley had found security and certainty; he was living in a steady home, one where time, interest and a genuine desire to do good for their grandson was being shown to him by his grandparents. Bradley was ingesting all the right ingredients to enable the reworking of his neural pathways thereby transmuting his feelings of worthlessness to those of self-worth. The hardened exterior shown in his school to his peers and teachers was beginning to soften because the affection and love he was experiencing in the kinship foster home was enabling a thawing of his frozen hidden emotional pain.

I shared that I had never been inside an allotment shed, but I had seen inside a garden shed. Bradley, with a sense of pride told me he had been in both. With no prompting from me he said he needed to make an allotment shed to stand on the clay allotment he was constructing. Here I provided some technical assistance at Bradley' request, because he had difficulty getting the slabs of clay needed for the walls of the shed to stand up.

However, the buckling walls of the construction gave the allotment shed plenty of character as well as an opportunity for Bradley and me to share ideas and thoughts about working with others and how good it felt to have someone to do things with. Bradley was communicating that he felt needed and valued by his Grandparents. There had not been too much eye contact as we built, but we were working cooperatively and purposefully. Together, we had invested time and energy into the making of the allotment shed and this gave value to the clay creation and the quality of our relationship.

I had seen Bradley's enjoyment when working with clay and could see that there was a connection between his pleasure in this and in digging the allotment — both were work with 'earthy' substances. Session four turned out to be an experimental one during which Bradley chose to make clay vegetables. The impetus for this occurred at the very beginning of the session when he took a lump of grey clay and separated it into two pieces. He did this through a tearing action and his attention was caught by the roughened surfaces the tearing had created. I was told about cabbages; the different types and when the seeds needed to be planted.

Next we experimented to see what other types of clay surface it was possible to make. Bradley showed me how he could make a kind of grass for the allotment by pushing small pieces of clay carefully through a kitchen sieve. In turn, I showed him how I could use a plastic knife to lightly scrape curls of clay away from the surface, as in scraping butter, to give the clay slab a surface like rock. We played together and had an enjoyable time.

Reflecting on this session afterwards, I could see that Bradley probably recognised he had my full attention as he talked and played with the clay. An appropriately interested adult spending time with a child naturally creates a bond, and, as we had played together, I had noted that we were fundamentally working on helping Bradley to foster the ability to form attachments. By doing this in the therapy session, the hope is that the child will be able to take this way of being into the outside world and work at developing better relationships there too.

Bradley continued to express his desire to work with clay for this certainly was his favoured medium in the therapy sessions. Continuing on the theme of the allotment, in the subsequent session Bradley spoke about seeing scarecrows on the allotments close to his step-grandfather's plot. This proved to be a rich subject, where Bradley and I shared some fascinating exchanges about the life of a scarecrow. Bradley expressed his worry that scarecrows were all alone in allotments or fields and how they often looked shabby and tatty.

He then went on to tell me about a story he had heard at school where the scarecrow had served his purpose by scaring away the crows and how amazing it was that he did his duty without needing any looking after by the farmer or his wife. All the while he was telling me this tale, Bradley was modelling in clay the scruffiest scarecrow imaginable! The metaphor of this story was significant, so we stayed with the scarecrow and the session passed by quickly. The storytelling part of working with clay is vital to understanding issues in a different way and in this session the created image was given little recognition ultimately for Bradley did not wish to keep the scarecrow. It had served its purpose and was no longer needed.

Asking if I knew what a gargoyle was, Bradley arrived ready for his seventh session. As I opened my mouth to reply, he excitedly told me gargoyles were for scaring evil spirits away.

I kept my mouth shut and regarded him saying, 'I see', after he'd finished.

'Let's make one. Can we?'

Again, I went to reply but it was not necessary due to Bradley diving straight into the clay bucket. I felt like a mother might do when a young child already knows what they need or want. So I simply followed Bradley's lead.

I settled down next to the table as Bradley prepared our working space by placing a large wooden board between us. Sitting with my chin in my hands, I watched as he began a tale about gargoyles. What a delight he was turning out to be. I relished his storytelling skills, accompanied by his animated movements — his face was often a sight to behold! I was being mesmerised, wooed into loving him, and I thought of Winnicott's theory (1971) that it is a baby's role to make the mother fall in love with her infant so the infant survives. This seemed to be just what was happening between Bradley and me. Right on cue, Bradley looked from the gargoyle face he had made, directly into mine.

'This gargoyle looks just like you!' he said as he fell about laughing!

'You cheeky monster,' I replied, which delighted him.

I had been expecting our work to carry on with the natural world theme, so was astonished when Bradley said in session seven that he would be making baby Jesus. This session was in early February, so the Christmas festivities were over, and there seemed to be little explanation for this big change in emphasis. But there was such a big change. I asked myself? Given the previous session had been the playful one, during which I had noticed a feeling of being 'wooed' by Bradley — wasn't it natural that now we were to see the baby itself!

How marvellous that the psyche knows what it needs to survive and thrive. Bradley deftly modelled an intricate baby's form, and then made a crib for it to rest in. My role, as this work got underway, was to watch. As I did so, I made comments quietly, for I was in awe of the emerging scene that conveyed

Clay Gargoyle

the symbolic concepts of hope and re-birthing. Winnicott's words echoed in my mind, 'It is only in being creative that the individual discovers the self' (1971, p. 54). This was just so true in the case of Bradley.

I was so disappointed that Bradley was unable to attend the next planned session due to him being ill. When non-attendance occurs straight after a profound session in which deep work has often taken place perhaps the psyche knows it requires a rest and an illness comes on.

The next time we were able to meet was three weeks later, due to the illness had preceded a mid-term break. When Bradley entered the therapy room he seemed changed, but I could not quite grasp how or why. We talked about the last remaining four sessions and what Bradley may wish to do in this time left to us. He appeared a little unsure how to start work with me, so, I helped the session along by offering a clay activity, having checked that he still wanted to work with clay.

I explained that the activity was making 'composite animals'. Bradley was not sure what I meant, so I invited him to follow what I was about to do in order that he could grasp how composite animals were made. This was veering away from how we had usually worked, in that there was more structure to the activity — I was interested in Bradley's reaction. He did not seem to mind.

We both had a lump of clay, which was subsequently broken into five pieces. First we chose one of the five pieces of clay to make an animal body. Once this was sculpted, we swapped bodies and used another piece of clay we made a head for our new body. Swapping these, we each now had our respective original clay bodies, so made legs for them. Swapping again, the instruction was to make a tail for the animal. On the fifth and final swap our task was to decorate the animal in any way that our last piece of clay seemed to suggest.

This activity took a long time due to the various stages, but at the end Bradley and I admired the co-created animals and he moved back into storytelling mode. There was no hesitation about wanting to keep the composite animals safely in his box. Co-creation is a powerful process that aids co-operation and bonding.

Initial hesitance seemed swept away, since in session ten Bradley beamingly informed we would be repeating the animal exercise from the previous week. This time, however, he was clear about wanting to take the lead. When each swap happened, Bradley instructed we should both add our part to an ongoing story. Creating in clay and remembering parts of the story took considerable concentration, resulting in both getting muddled, but this was quite tolerable to Bradley, for the confidence he had gained in our work together allowed for mistakes to happen. He told me it was similar to playing a game of consequences. Now I could definitely see there had been a shift in Bradley's emotional make-up. He was gradually acquiring a belief in himself.

Session eleven arrived and Bradley suggested he had a look at everything in his box. He took out his clay work from the different sessions and my role was to help him place them on the table in chronological sequence. I reminded myself how important the therapists' function is in 'holding' the memory of the work and this was a good example of the worthwhile process. Here, before Bradley and I, was evidence of the time we had spent together and the work we had done. As each clay model came out of the box, a narrative accompanied explaining how it had been made and what the difficulties had been. This really was quite a sophisticated process. In this pen-ultimate session we were having a review of the therapeutic process but more significantly, it had been instigated by Bradley.

As the remembering and narration came to a close, it was decided Bradley would bring in a wooden crate from the allotment, so he could take home his creations in the last session.

I had not wanted the final session to come because I was reluctant for Bradley to take away his clay images. In the making process I had become attached to the creations as I had to Bradley. Bradley arrived cheerfully carrying the promised wooden crate which contained newspapers. He informed me his grandmother had suggested he bring the newspapers for wrapping his clay models in. Out came Bradley's box again and this time the clay works were removed and placed on the table without any storytelling accompaniment. This, therefore, was not a ritual as in session eleven, but a closing of the work, as each clay model was wrapped in newspaper. Everything was wrapped. Nothing was discarded. All was going home with Bradley.

It had been a poignant last session where and I was moved when Bradley gave me a goodbye hug as his grandfather carried the clay work to the waiting car. It had been good work and I was left in reverence at the thought that children show such resilience in the will to survive.

Discussion

Surprised by how swiftly the therapeutic relationship had been built, I realised how badly needed the therapeutic input had been. As Bradley worked on the clay allotment and shed within the first three sessions, a strong foundation for future therapeutic work was established. Bradley continued to use clay often in the remaining sessions and would speak freely about visits from his mother and how he missed his siblings and father, because an understanding between us had been co-created. A trusting relationship had been formed that would emotionally support this young gardener-in-the-making. I reminded myself that the supportive investment the grandparents were making in Bradley outside of therapy had helped immeasurably in enabling this secure attachment process.

Naturally, there were likely to be lapses when Bradley felt less secure because of his earlier life experiences, but, fundamentally, something strongly positive had been taking root and was growing through the safe and steady environment the grandparent's home afforded.

Chapter 10

Bereavement: Katriona (age 10)

Reasons for Selecting this Case

A case study illustrating the use of clay with bereavement issues has the potential to offer the ultimate in therapeutic existential perspective, for human matter is derived from the body of the earth. That is to say, our earthly body is composed of minerals and water hence the connection with Mother Earth is at an absolutely fundamental level. In scientific and philosophical terms humans would not exist if it was not for planet earth. This line of thinking then leads back to the Jungian concept that the earth is the root of all. (Schwartz-Salant (ed.), 1995). Hence working with clay, an earthy substance, offers a profound experience when working with notions of birth and death. We come from the earth and we return to the earth: 'ashes to ashes, dust to dust'.

However, this case study is a paradox in itself, for the irony of it is that the therapeutic work was carried out using air-dry clay! Air-drying clay is synthetic clay and therefore man-made. Are not humans made by humans, but still the human body is made of the earth's compounds? Such are the thought-provoking parallels of this case.

Prior to commencing the therapy work with the client at the centre of this study, I had been discussing with a supervisee the properties of real clay and air-drying clay. Having worked with the air-drying clay in the supervision session I had inadvertently left this clay bag next to the bucket of real clay. The client had selected the air-drying clay and I was not about to decline the choice; so presents the conundrum! It is a useful opportunity to include a case study where synthetic clay was used.

Introduction

The finality of death is hard for adults to accept and assimilate into their everyday understanding of life and its meaning. Theories of bereavement from a child's perspective suggest that it is around the age of 8 that children are able to comprehend the concept of death. However, it is essential to consider each child as an individual whose own psychological and intellectual development naturally come into play, as well as the life experiences of the particular child. Youngsters who have looked after a pet fish, hamster, cat or dog probably have had some exposure to a pet's death and hopefully will have been included and involved in the funeral of such, when parents and carers have been available to answer pertinent questions on what happens to the pet when it dies.

World and national disasters, whilst usually occurring at a geographical distance nevertheless can have an impact on children and adolescents. Media images bring traumatic scenes directly to youngsters, and feelings of fear and confusion are not uncommon when young people begin to consider whether frightening events could happen closer to home.

In school settings children sometimes hear about the death of a peer or adult such as a member of staff, and this again may shake their confidence and comprehension of a secure world. However, when the death is of a significant family member, this has a profound effect on a child. Depression in young adult males may often have roots in the awful experience of an early childhood bereavement that has not been worked through.

Depression and grief may present as very similar in children and adolescents. Sadness and grief are absolutely natural responses to being bereft. Freud (1917) recognised sadness as a normal human response to loss, calling the phenomena 'melancholy'. If appropriate support within the family and community is available to a bereaved child or adolescent the sadness hopefully can be understood, accepted and held. It is heartening to note many counties within the United Kingdom have bereavement services available for families to seek additional support for cases when the death has been sudden and unexpected.

When details surrounding the case are horrific, the grief process may become pathological, causing children and adolescents to present as emotionally withdrawn, shut down or frozen.

We hear of families being unable to speak of the death, families separating, families quarrelling, and so on, when the circumstances associated with the death are just too painful to work through. This makes it almost impossible for the child or adolescent to fully grieve.

The experiences of working with bereaved young people has pointed the way to mainly adopting an open, 'continuing bonds' model of grief when the relationship to the deceased has been a good one. This means helping to foster an ongoing appreciation of the deceased. By using the word 'appreciation', the intention is not to solely identify the positive attributes and memories of the deceased, but rather to help and support the client in identifying the not-so-positive, thus building a closer true-to-life construct so the person can be remembered and internalised in totality.

Whilst acknowledging these ideas work well in a family that is not beset with additional difficulties, many therapists will be working with younger clients where this is not the case. These cases with additional difficulties are more complex, and the bereavement may become secondary to the main referral reason or completely lost in unravelling of the concerns.

Case Background Information

Katriona, the eldest of four children, was a 10-year-old client who came into therapy because her maternal grandmother had recently died. The grandmother had lived with the family for many years and her role had been as a mother's help for she had almost raised the children when Katriona's mother had been working at a local hospital catering department. Both Katriona's parents lived at home, so the household had previously been a busy and hectic one, as described by Katriona's mother.

The loss of the grandmother had necessitated a change in the parents' working days. Katriona's mother had become concerned and distressed with her eldest daughter's constant clingy behaviour and she felt Katriona's sadness and tears at bed time were going on too long. She voiced that Katriona should be over the death of her grandmother. It became apparent that Katriona's mother was struggling with the difficulties the death of her mother had brought about, which necessitated having to change her working day and then being around her children so much more.

However, there was a sense that Katriona's needs were being overlooked through this difficult family time. I noted Katriona's early years had been described in positive terms and deduced the family had functioned reasonably well, thereby laying the foundations for sound personality development. Given that it appeared Katriona's emotional needs as a young child had probably been met, it seemed safe to assume counselling sessions could focus on bereavement, as opposed to developmental work, with perhaps some structure being given to the individual sessions. As a result it was agreed an eight-week counselling contract would be offered to Katriona.

Therapeutic Work

This case study will focus on the last four sessions of the contract, because this was when Katriona asked specifically to work with clay, however, to set the study in context the first session is briefly covered below.

The first session began well, with Katriona sharing quite openly that she knew she had come to talk about her Nan's death caused by breast cancer. Nan apparently had been ill for several years and when she received chemotherapy treatment Katriona was only too keenly aware of the physical impact on her Nan. This meant Katriona needed to be especially considerate to her Nan following periods of treatment.

As explained above, air-dry clay was used when, in the fifth session, the therapeutic work noticeably deepened and appeared to quicken in pace. Katriona possessed advanced mathematical skills and knowledge, so after flattening a lump of clay by rolling it out, she asked for paper and scissors. Selecting a piece of A4 paper, she folded it lengthways and set about cutting out a heart shape. Using the paper heart as a template, Katriona pressed it gently into the slab of clay with her fingers and then, with precision, cut around the heart. This is not an easy shape to cut from a slab of clay and Katriona was dissatisfied with some edges. To rectify the slightly unevenness of some, she smoothed these carefully with her thumb, checking her work intently to ensure the clay heart was to her liking; then she stepped back from the clay image. Not wishing to disturb the moment more than necesssary, I said,

'Katriona, you seem to be thinking about the heart.'

'Um, I don't know what to do with it. I want it to be in two pieces.'
I nodded in response to Katriona and waited until she was ready.

'Shall I cut it down the middle in a straight line, or shall I do a zigzag cut through the middle?'

She appeared to be asking herself this question, in a hushed voice, and so I enquired gently:

'What does it seem you want to do most?'

'I want to do a zigzag line.'
Having made this decision, she began diligently to cut a vertical zigzag with a blunt plastic knife through the clay heart.

This was a difficult scene to witness. Was this Katriona's heart I wondered? It was important that I maintained a tracking focus. Tilting my head as Katriona's cutting actions changed direction, I watched the zigzag line progress. I was hoping Katriona would register the interest I was taking in her activity, because the work so clearly seemed to express something that was close to the heart, metaphorically speaking. Looking at the clay heart that was now in two pieces the word 'broken-hearted' came to mind. Katriona then identified the clay image.

'This is my mum's broken heart. Her heart is breaking 'cos Nan has died. It is horrible watching her cry. She thinks I don't know she is crying, but I do. I hear her sniffing when she thinks I'm not close by her. I know she's been crying because her red eyes tell me. Sometimes when she cries I get frightened and I cry too. Then mum hears me and tells me not to cry. She says that when we get older our parents die and I asked her if she was going to die. She said one day she would and that's scaring me. I don't want her to die and I don't want to get older either.'

The clay heart was suddenly forgotten, as we changed track and began to consider what it meant for Katriona to get older. We talked about the many experiences Katriona may have. We spoke about the family that Katriona was part of and we talked about having both good and not so good memories. This discussionn was helped by mentioning the death of family pets and I disclosed how I had felt about my dog dying. Katriona seemed to appreciate hearing memories about how my dog had done a few disastrous things when she had been a puppy, such as trying to squeeze through a cat-flap in a door but getting stuck.

My wondering out loud what Katriona remembered about her Nan took Katriona to a thoughtful place. She shared how good Nan's apple and blackberry crumbles had been and how Nan could get very cross with Katriona's granddad for walking into the kitchen still wearing his muddy work boots. Katriona also remembered Nan always buying her white chocolate when she was a toddler, because when eating milk chocolate Katriona had got her clothes very messy. At this Katriona looked down at the clay heart, then smiled up at me and said the clay was a similar colour to white chocolate for air-drying clay generally is paler in colour.

We sat for a few moments smiling at each other. It was one of those beautiful points in therapy when our gazes locked and we were together in the moment. When this happens there can be a reluctance to break the spell of togetherness. However, the session was drawing to a close and I asked what Katriona wanted to do with the heart. Perhaps I had realised intuitively this clay piece was highly significant, because Katriona asking for it to be air-dried so she could paint it the following week.

Katriona arrived for session six requesting to see the heart straight away, because she wanted to know what it now looked like one week later. She pushed the two halves together to shape a complete heart and repeated this movement several times. Next she turned the two pieces over and performed the same movements, but this time her actions were more gentle.

Katriona seemed to be in a world of her own, so I made no interruption; such a trance-like state, even if only momentarily, allows the client to dip deeply into the personal and sometimes collective unconscious. The dream-like state seems to suspend thinking in the moment, offering a relaxed condition in which images and concepts naturally flow, thereby connecting the individual with the archetypal world. I surmised Katriona was in touch with the anima: the psychic personification of the feminine principle. As we were working with three generations of females within the same family I appreciated the significance here of the matriarchal aspect, representing the three stages of girl, mother and old woman.

After moving the two heart pieces around Katriona decided to paint the air-dried clay heart. She spent some ten minutes or so choosing, pouring and mixing various colours from the three tubes of primary poster paints namely blue, red and yellow. Black and white were also available, as were gold, silver and copper. Limiting the colours available in the therapy room encourages clients to experiment with mixing to create shades and hues that reverberate personally.

Katriona was no exception in her absorption into making her own potions and colours, although it is unusual to see such a sophisticated process of mixing as hers, in which the strong deep pink lightened to a paler pink and faded out to almost a mere hint of pink in the white. These colours seemed to suggest a mood of being alive, then fading to a deadening ghostly white. When the top of the two halves of the heart had been completed blood red, the red paint was then used to carefully paint the edges and back of the heart shapes. This painting of the heart was indeed a work of art that I had the privilege to witness.

It became abundantly clear how my role was to be that of an appreciative onlooker to the purity of her creation, only moving when required to do so in assisting the work in progress. Deep was the absorption of both of us. Something profound and sacred was unfolding, and in the quietness of this activity we were sharing I wondered about the transmuting powers of the work. The alchemical process of changing dull, grey matter into a bright object d'art is something quite special; something golden was transpiring.

Katriona spotted the silver poster paint pot and, working quickly, she painted over the blood-red edges of the heart with the silver paint. All this took place with graceful movements. Then, as if she had set eyes upon treasure, when she spied the gold paint her facial expression gave way to sheer joy. For a 10-year-old to show such an incredible level of manual dexterity when engaged in painting is also pure delight for the therapist to witness, especially in this case when the gold was meticulously applied to the inside edges of the zigzag cuts.

Many a therapist might frown at another giving praise to a work of art emerging in a therapy session, but in this moment, I could not refrain from doing so. I was mesmerised. 'Wow!' I was almost shaking my head in disbelief at the beauty of the heart that had been created.

Moving together, as if in a dance, Katriona and I lent forward over the clay work cradled in her hand. When Katriona sat back to view the creation, checking how it looked from different angles, then admiring the model, I did the same. The pleasure of the experience we shared in the moment flowed between therapist and client. The beauty that was felt in the relationship was the 'magic medicine' where creativity, the arts and the profoundly sacred were the potent ingredients. It was a shame to end the session, for when two minds come together meeting at a deep level something of a healing nature is distilled.

Following the painting of the heart session, Katriona's mother telephoned informing how she felt much relief that Katriona seemed much improved, even though the course of therapy was not completed. This feedback is valuable to therapists and it is always worth reflecting on anything of special note that may have taken place in the session prior to the parental contact.

Early in the seventh session the painted clay heart was viewed appreciatively then wrapped in bright yellow tissue paper. The heart obviously still held much meaning; the importance of it was still alive with potential, and this highlighted that it had become a powerful symbol for Katriona. Interestingly, Katriona spoke of making flags and banners at school while decorating her classroom to mark the occasion of the monarch's jubilee celebrations. I wondered at the connection between the heart-making and flag-making activities, for this association evidently had some meaning.

Next Katriona moved to cut a small piece of clay and began rolling it thinly on a wooden board. I could see straight away that the clay was not performing to Katriona's liking and this did not suit her. She used a plastic spatula to scrape the thin layer of clay from the board, but this only caused further problems. The more effort Katriona put into removing the clay, the more it tore. In a quandary, I wondered how long I should stand back from the situation.

'Heck, we have a problem!" Katriona sat back in her chair quite deflated and her spirit seemed crushed.

Choosing this moment to think aloud I said, 'I get mad when I'm frustrated that things don't go the way I need them to. You know, sometimes it's Okay but sometimes it's not.'

For the therapist, it is necessary to know when enough has been said. When feeling uncertain, the golden rule is, it is better to say less than too much.

With a slightly defensive position Katriona pulled herself forward and lethargically tossed the clay around on the board. Time seemed to stand still while I sat motionless waiting to see what would unfold in this space of potential. Katriona seemed to muster some mild enthusiasm, as if a new idea had come to mind. Pulling a funny face, she shared she was going to make a clay banner. This idea sounded complicated and I was intrigued as to how Katriona was going to implement it.

She next reached for a piece of paper and smartly cut out a heart-shaped template, though smaller than the one she had made in session five, saying she would use this for cutting out lots of clay hearts. Due to the clay being unresponsive to the previous rolling out process, Katriona decided to squash small pieces of clay in the palms of her hands. Whilst this meant each squashed piece of clay was a slightly different thickness, she did not seem perturbed. Laying the flattened clay pieces on a board and using the paper template, she proceeded to cut five clay hearts out.

Clay Hearts

The undulating clay hearts were not uniform. Again, a quizzical look crossed Katriona's face and I responded with a questioning raise of the eyebrows. I could see she was now deep in thought, so I waited, not wishing to hurry the process for there was certainly a transmuting process taking place. Katriona bent over the clay hearts, then she carefully picked one up and started to pull it into a less symmetrical shape. I moved my position to give me a better view of what her actions. She looked up at me as she laid this heart down. With more energy she then made the other four hearts asymmetrical ones then pushed a hole into all five.

The session was rapidly coming to an end and I quietly reminded Katriona that the next session would be our last meeting. She nodded, conveying her understanding, and requested that the collage box, housing interesting bits and pieces of paper, card and cloth be ready for her.

In the final session Katriona laid the hearts on a wooden board saying she was going to paint them ready to take home. She started mixing pink and then used most of the session to experiment with mixing variations of pinks, creams and yellows. All sides of the hearts were to be painted, which meant I was required to be on hand for technical support in holding up the hearts as Katriona decorated them. When each heart had dried, a quick squirt of gold and silver paint was sprayed to produce a dazzling effect. Katriona was thrilled at what was happening with the five small hearts.

To complete the work Katriona rummaged in the collage box, pulling out a ball of brown string. She wanted red, but this could not be found. Sometimes, therapists just do not have what the client wants and in the session with Katriona I worked with this, reflecting that this is similar to real, everyday life situations. She appeared to be listening as she worked at using the string to connect the hearts together like bunting. I was a little concerned about the potential for the hearts to get broken when suspended in this way, but the concern was mine and not Katriona's whose excitement was contagious.

One of the last comments from Katriona was that now everyone in the family had a heart. This was an evocative and powerful comment from her. The ending was a good one, with

Katriona's mother responding appreciatively to her daughter's enthusiasm when showing her clay pieces.

When mother and daughter had left I sat quietly musing on the thought that the Queen's jubilee celebrations had been marked by fluttering fabric buntings, whilst Katriona had marked the passing of her grandmother by making solid hearts. Two matriarchal events had been marked in a short space of time, though in different ways.

Discussion

The therapy work had gone well with Katriona, and it was heartening to look back over the contracted time and realise this, for it cannot be said for all work. The identified, specific focus of the work that a death in the family had created enabled a natural flow which the tangible outcome meant there was little need for associations or interpretations to be made.The created clay images spoke for themselves, with the symbolic meaning being richly personal. That said, the importance of hearts is acknowledges the world over.

The love felt in the heart from her grandmother was going to be an enduring emotion for Katriona, so in a sense, the fact that she selected air-drying clay seemed meant to be and not an accident. With air-drying clay there was less chance the creation would break. Whereas if natural clay had been used, the hardening fragility of the medium could have caused breakage and emotional pain. As it was, the air-drying clay suited the purpose and the work well, even though Katriona got a little agitated with the texture of it sometimes.

PART THREE

CLAY THERAPY
with Adolescents: Case Studies

Chapter 11

Parent imprisonment:
Logan (age 12)

Reasons for Selecting this Case

The main aim for including the case study on Logan is to expand thinking on children and adolescents who may be referred for therapy when there is an undiagnosed condition that other professionals consider could be classed as oppositional defiant behaviour. Heeding the reasons for referral is essential although working with the troubled youngster is more important.

A further reason for writing this study is to illustrate how therapeutic work does happen even when there are only a few sessions, but also to show the impact an unplanned, abrupt ending may have on a therapist. Unfortunately, it was not possible to include photographic material with this case due to the spontaneous actions explained in the latter part of this chapter.

Introduction

The impact of parental imprisonment upon a young person is such that for some children they almost seem to be suffering for the parent's crime. Children speak of the stigma attached to a parent being sentenced to spend time in prison and how they face many difficulties, such as maintaining contact with the imprisoned parent. Instability, broken family relationships and peer difficulties are some of the main concerns that young people speak of in therapy, whilst I have also noted developmental progress may be hampered. Children of an imprisoned parent can therefore be at risk educationally and socially. However, for some youngsters having a parent in prison can be a relief and when a release date is known this sometimes leads to huge anxiety. Much depends upon the crime the parent has committed.

Case Background Information

A local school behavioural support unit made contact enquiring if I would accept a referral to work with a 12-year-old 'wild child', as Logan was called. He was proving very difficult to manage in the unit and when he attended, which was sporadic, he caused mayhem amongst his peers. The staff were becoming weary of his outbursts, since the level of disruption Logan was creating was too much for the unit to accommodate.

I accepted the referral saying I would meet with Logan and his mother initially to assess if therapeutic work would be beneficial at this point. Having heard from the unit that Logan's father was imprisoned six months ago for grievous bodily harm I wanted to have more information before commencing the work for this potentially could be a challenging case.

Logan and his mother arrived on time for our meeting. Both seemed dishevelled and irritated with each other. Logan's mother appeared a troubled woman, having been subjected to domestic violence by several partners since Logan's father had left the marital home some eight years earlier. I had hoped to meet Logan's mother on her own but the staff at the behavioural unit had relayed her reluctance to do this. I surmised that perhaps Logan was the 'man of the house', for in the meeting with the three of us he was certainly very vocal.

In his presence, his mother seemed timid and unable to make herself heard without Logan interrupting with his huffing or animalistic noises, or simply just talking right over what she was trying to say. Here it was necessary to work as a mediator so both sides of the story could be told. Cases like this are tricky to manage in first meetings, so it was necessary to work hard at keeping the focus on what Logan's needs were for the moment, whist simultaneously gathering information that would assist in assessing what issues might require monitoring.

At the end of the meeting I felt tired. Much energy had been needed to hold the meeting together to maintain a modicum of decency, whilst also concentrating on the unfolding family story. Yes, Logan did seem pretty wild. But, more than that, he was an angry adolescent who underneath the aggressive exterior, was hurting like mad. I did not dismiss the opinion of the behavioural unit staff that Logan should be diagnosed with oppositional defiant disorder, but since I an not trained to medically diagnose such things I was far more interested in the personal story.

A short contract was set to work with Logan, because the long summer break was only six weeks away. Knowing of Logan's erratic attendance at the unit, I stressed how important it was for him to attend our sessions for the six weeks; after which we could review the situation. He begrudgingly agreed to come for the six sessions and I went on to explain the limits of confidentiality and my working boundaries: to keep Logan safe, me safe and the room safe, This straightforward phrase usually proves helpful should a session get out of hand.

Therapeutic Work

I was ready at four o'clock to meet Logan for our first appointment. He was ten minutes late, muttering he did not want to see a 'shrink' and that no one could make him. I stated that I, too, did not like being made to do things and preferred to have a choice. That stopped him in his tracks. He looked straight into my eyes and said, "You seem normal!" I think I grimaced as my thoughts took me back to my mother's comments about me being weird because I was arty! Logan huffed at my grimace. Straight away I knew I would need to be mindful in not colluding with the non-conformist elements in his character.

'Where's yer computer?' questioned Logan. I explained I did not use a computer in therapy sessions.

'Why not?'

'I work with other materials such as charcoal, chalk, paints, the sandtray or clay.'

'Then why have yer got puppets in ere?' retorted Logan.

'I use puppets too sometimes,' I said. Logan was unimpressed.

'Well I'm not bloody playing with puppets. They're for play-group kids. What d'ya think I am? I hate drawing. I can't paint. It's like school. This is going to be boring. What time can I go?'

'So you don't think much to this therapy business then Logan.' Logan ignored my comment.

'Yer got loads clay in that bucket. Reckon you got six kilograms there. Yer sort of got about twelve bags worth of sugar in that bucket. That's a lot of clay!'

With that he yanked the lid off the clay bucket and peered in.

'God it's messy. Don't you get dirty with all this? Do kids throw it at you?'

I managed to squeeze in a reply before he rattled off any more questions.

'This clay is for making what you want to. You can decide what you want to make. It's your choice!.'

Pulling some clay out of the bucket Logan began smashing his hand into it.

'I need more!'

I nodded at Logan's statement, watching as he shoved his right hand deep into the clay. The bucket toppled over at the force he used.

'I want all the clay out.'

I reached for a large wooden board, thinking this would be a good base on which to work, but then the thought flashed through my mind that Logan's energy could spill out anywhere.

'Just a minute whilst I lay down this large plastic sheet on the floor.'

Logan co-operated with this request and even helped when I started to flatten it. He positioned some large pebbles at the corners of the sheeting to anchor it down — this being his initiative.

'Okay, now we're ready.'

I was somewhat surprised at Logan's readiness to help; he was not being difficult or awkward. In fact, we had just started working cooperating on something and this had to be a plus, following our first verbal exchanges. I thanked him for his help.

'S'alright mate!' came his reply.

With a questioning look that suggested he was testing me, Logan next pulled all the clay from the bucket. This was no mean feat, for getting 12lbs of clay out from a container is hard work. But, grasping and puffing, Logan doggedly carried out his intention.

'It's hard work. Looks like you're pretty determined though,' I commented.

'Yer right, it's bloody hard work. I'll beat the hell out of it!' Logan huffed.

Quite frankly, the rest of the session felt like a pantomime as Logan pulled, huffed, swore and scuttled round on the plastic sheeting with the bucket and the clay. He certainly was wrestling with something and I felt as if I was the referee. At some point I mentioned he should take care, because as I thought Logan could hurt his hand if he carried on punching the clay with such venom. He guffawed back.

'No one cares if I get hurt.'

'I do Logan.'

'Why? Yer just saying that. That's yer job.'

'It is my job to make sure you don't hurt yourself in here, but I do care if you get hurt.'

At that Logan grunted and carried on punching the clay although with a little less vigour I thought.

Although the 12lb heap of clay looked robust enough and stood up to the beating it had just received, it was a little worse for wear. Having dried out somewhat with the heat in the room, it had also begun to crack. When Logan finally seemed to have spent his energy, I mentioned he had reminded me of a boxer fighting an opponent.

'Did I?' he asked in a pleased voice.

I was not sure if this had been necessarily the best response from me, but it was the one I had chosen and I'd have to live with it. However, Logan went with the idea and made an association telling me his father was in prison for beating people up. He went on to say his mother suffered with her nerves because she was forever getting stressed out over nothing in his view. Never-the-less, he was worried about her because she needed to work long hours to bring money in due to some state benefits being reduced.

As the session came to a close, Logan checked what I would be doing with the clay he had used. I explained that because it had been used well it would need a rest. Quizzically he looked at me.

'Where's it gonna rest?' I thought for a moment before replying. When clay has been so well used there is a disinclination on my part to recycle it, but it does seem important to provide the client with a choice about what they want to happen to the medium. Logan had shown an unusual interest with his question and I needed to quickly decide how best to answer.

'It could rest in the bucket or, we could put it to rest in the ground; after all, that's where clay comes from.'

'Can I do it?' came the instant reply.

'You want to put it back into the ground where it will become part of the earth again,' I checked.

Logan genuinely seemed to like this idea as he shared his appreciation with me of being eco-friendly. Fortunately, the office I worked in was surrounded by a small, private garden and (ever mindful of not having session boundaries compromised) I spoke to Logan about needing to stay within the garden fence. He was absolutely fine with this, so we struggled between us to lift the clay, still on the plastic sheeting, and move it outside.

Logan was sharp to spot a place where he wanted the clay to go once we were in the garden: he saw a shady corner under a eucalyptus where some ferns were growing and nodded his head in that direction. I had thought perhaps he would need a trowel or shovel to dig with, but he went down on his knees and dug bare-handed to make a hollow for the clay to rest in. I was quite fascinated by what seemed like the actions of a forager living close to nature. Once satisfied with the size of the hollow, Logan took a deep breath, lifted the clay and placed it reverently into the ground. He then gently covered the clay over with a thin layer of soil. Wiping his dirty hands on the slightly damp grass, he told me he would be back next week to do more clay work.

In my notes I recorded how the first session had been an astonishing one that I could not have envisaged. I had felt I had been working with an almost semi-feral child, but yet one who seemed to have his wits about him; he had seen life.

'H'ya Lynne, have you got more clay this week?' Logan asked as he bounded through the office door right on time for the second session. There were no formal greetings with Logan, for he was ready to work immediately. He told me he was going to make a prison block from the clay, going on to mention he had visited his father in prison over the weekend, but because the prison was a long way off he knew he would not be going again soon. I nodded my understanding of this as Logan set about rolling the clay bucket on its side in readiness to pull the clay out. Swiftly, the large plastic sheet was laid on the floor. This time the clay fell out of the bucket easily, still inside the plastic bag that helped to keep it moist. Logan was irritated by this and roughly ripped the polythene away to expose the raw clay. Again, we were working with a lump of clay about 12lbs in weight, and for a thin, wiry youngster it takes energy to move around a lump of earth this heavy. Logan got down on his haunches in order to shove and push the clay into a form that he wanted. He was not happy that the clay was resisting his physical attempts and became frustrated. He sat back on his bottom with an air of resignation.

'Nothing ever works!' He gave the clay a hard kick. The clay rebuffed his action. We looked at each other and I waited for what might unfold. I looked at the clay, then at Logan, then at the clay again, still saying nothing. Logan shifted so he was kneeling on one knee and bent down closer to the clay to study the dent his foot had made. Now on both knees he used a clenched fist to enlarge the dent. He then opened his hand out so he could use the palm and fingers to smooth the concave shape in the clay. He needed to steady the bulk of the clay with his other hand and these actions clearly were drawing a great deal of effort and energy from Logan.

He stopped to rest every now and again, and it seemed to me as if Logan was thinking something through; soon enough I learned he intended now to make a cave. Thus, the initial idea of making a prison block had transformed into a cave creation. Logan had not required my assistance, which afforded an opportunity to fully witness and track what was happening in this session. I silently considered the fact that Logan's process had moved from a theme of imprisonment to one of protection — and wondered where this work was taking him.

It can be quite staggering how quickly the time goes to in a therapy session. This certainly was the case with Logan, because soon we were at the end of the second session and I was faced with finding somewhere to keep the clay moist for a week, so that Logan would be able to work on it in session three, as he had requested.

After he had left I had trouble locating a box big enough to house the cave for a week, so I wrapped it up in polythene to ensure no air could get to the clay. Upon entering the room for session three, Logan saw the great big messy parcel and was not impressed, scoffing at my efforts at wrapping up his cave. He was not being defiant or oppositional — just darn right honest! Logan was the sort of youngster who called a spade, a spade. We both studied the mass of polythene and damp clay, then:

'Yer rubbish at this!' he boldly observed.

I had been expecting his comment.

Feeling deflated, I responded flatly, 'You think I'm rubbish.'

It had been a statement, not a question, but the response from Logan was quite touching.

'Na, yer not rubbish, yer just no good at wrapping up.'

'Oh, I see.'

I turned to look at him and, surprisingly I was looking into the face of a youngster showing some sympathy. I gave a slight smile.

'Yeah!' I said.

In that short interchange two minds met in the understanding that both knew it can be painful to be criticised; and I had a sense that the unspoken words between us intimated we were in this work together, working properly in tandem!

From that moment onwards I felt like a comrade. I use the word 'comrade' deliberately, for what happened afterwards moved us into working harmoniously. Together we laid flat the large plastic sheet on the floor. The unwrapped cave was placed on the sheet with the entrance facing us. Finding the pebbles again, Logan this time positioned some large ones near the cave entrance, whilst using smaller ones to line a path. Now he told me he needed a river. Some discussion took place as to how a river could be made, and Logan demonstrated his resourcefulness by cutting away some clay from the back of the cave and modelling river banks; that is to say, he found what he needed.

When he poured water into the 'river' it naturally flowed out in both directions because there was nothing to stop it. I pondered the idea that Logan's experiences in his early years had probably not been 'contained'.

'Quick, do something!' Logan yelled.

'What shall I do Logan?'

'Dunno, but stop the water, stop the water, stop, stop, stop!' he wailed.

By now the office floor was wet, not flooded, but wet, and Logan looked worried. I know I looked puzzled. All of this had happened so quickly that I had not had time to stop the overflow, but what I did do next was to let Logan know it was my job to cope with the puddles at either end of the 'river'. It is always hard to know when to halt actions in a session, but I was thankful I had not stopped the flow of the work for in this hiccup there was meaning.

Reaching for a couple of cleaning cloths, I began mopping up the flow on the floor at one end of the river. At the same time Logan did the same at the other end, but his cloth brushed up against the, by now, slopping wet clay river banks. This resulted in the cloth becoming saturated with very wet, slippery clay. Logan was in his element. The cloth was a mess and his hands were covered in runny clay. He slightly lost his balance, which meant one hand landed on the river bank, smearing the clay further on the plastic sheet. He liked the effect and put his other hand into the sludge, smearing lots of runny clay towards the cave entrance.

'Look at this Lynne. D'ya like it?'

When I mentioned the session needed to end in five minutes time, Logan was not happy, I pushed further, however, asking what he'd like to do with the scene that had been created and explained keeping it would be difficult. We came to a joint decision that the cave and river scene could be photographed, so Logan could see it again in the fourth session. Also that he would trust me to recycle the clay after taking the photograph.

What a session this third one had been! Active, fast flowing, much being worked through, the togetherness! It had been absolutely essential to contain the work through 'holding the boundaries'. The overspill of water had seemed like a gift in the session after all. Accidents happen, but worked with and working together, they can be fixed. The result can be more than a fix, if it gives rise, to further creativity.

Ensuring there was a full bucket of clay ready for the fourth session I eagerly awaited Logan's arrival at four o'clock. Four o'clock came, but there was no Logan. Fifteen minutes later Logan had still not arrived. By now I was beginning to feel concern. I had not received a message from the school unit informing me that Logan would not be attending. I sat in my office feeling gloomy. The gloominess turned to sadness as I waited for Logan. I decided I would make telephone contact with Logan's home but there was no reply. I telephoned Logan's school unit only to be met with an answerphone message.

Reflecting on the predicament, I pondered when I had been in a similar situation. Each scenario that scrolled through my mind did not echo the loss I was feeling that day until I recognised the main feeling was one of being let down, not by anyone in particular. I considered if I felt let down by Logan, but concluded this was not the case; however, I was disappointed not to see him. I realised that the feeling was of an old, childhood disappointment. Just as I was making a new friend,

I, or the friend, would be moved to another county or country, such was the life of a child whose parent was engaged in a transient profession.

The following day I spoke with the school unit referrer who told me Logan's family had apparently moved to another area, to be nearer the prison where his father was an inmate. The unit had not been given notice of Logan's departure, which had been as abrupt for them as it had for me. Here. I recognised the echo of those old loses from my early years; however then, unlike now, I had generally been given some warning that the loss would occur.

Discussion

I had enjoyed the masculine ways of being Logan had brought to our sessions, for it had touched on the animus principles that had encompassed my childhood years. Logan's world echoed my glimpses of combat and the existential notions of fear of death and survival, whilst simultaneously strengthening levels of resilience within.

Clients leave suddenly at times, with no reason being given, and this can cause our personal experiences of loss to reverberate. When writing this case study personal experiences of compounded losses from childhood surfaced, and I appreciated again where my compassion while working with troubled children and adolescents has its roots. The accompanying sadness needed to be acknowledged and so I reminded myself to go gently as my own forgotten memories surfaced. The impact of children's and adolescents' experiences should never be underestimated, for they can last a lifetime.

Chapter 12

Bullying:
Jodie (age 13)

Reasons for Selecting this Case

Strong emotions of shame and humiliation have a negative impact on self-esteem and are at times difficult to detect, yet may reverberate in the therapeutic work. Clay therapy offers the chance to exhume these elusive emotions, giving form to the worries by making them visible. Viewing images makes it easier to share thoughts about the worries with another. Children and adolescents find talking about bullying difficult to initiate, often because it is hard to pinpoint what the difficulties are, particularly when the bullying is of a psychological nature. Secrecy is often a vital ingredient in fascilitating bullying behaviour. Once it is possible to put into words what has been taking place, the feeling of isolation diminishes.

Introduction

Bullying is insidious, often having long lasting effects on youngsters who experience it. In my work as a secondary school teacher I saw firsthand the awful impact bullying actions had for those on the receiving end. The result was that my responsibilities as a child protection coordinator were extended to include writing an anti-bullying policy that was active and alive in the school. Too many such policies were written and stored safely in a filing cabinet, only to see the light of day when a school inspection was underway. As a clinical supervisor and therapy educator, I understand this situation has since changed.

Policies do not stop bullying behaviour, but provide an

opportunity in the writing of them to consider why bullying actions occur and what prompts one person to attempt to intimidate and dominate another. The reality of the misuse of power and notions of dominance and subservience can be seen throughout the world in most cultures and, historically, this has led to devastating consequences on a dreadful scale. For a small child or vulnerable adolescent threatened by bullying behaviour, the consequences can be dire. The resulting feelings lead to being shamed and humiliated. Self-esteem and personal views of worth then implode.

Case Background Information

Jodie, a 13-year-old girl attending a grammar school where entrance to the educational establishment was through a selective academic examination, made a request to her parents for help in coping with sad feelings. Jodie's parents were concerned at their daughter's daily reluctance to go to school and her withdrawal from wanting to mix with peers for extra curricula activities.

When I first met with her parents, Jodie's father appeared a quiet man with little to say and yet his presence within the room suggested he was a traditional father, remaining aloof from his wife's worries about their daughter. I learned he had worked long and hard hours to establish a business that was struggling financially in an uncertain economic climate. Perhaps he was preoccupied with his own worries, but the fact was he seemed to be somewhat distant at our meeting. I wondered if he was not emotionally available to support the family and what the consequences of this could be for them, admittedly his presence showed his concern. Jodie's mother on the other hand, offered helpful information and clearly wanted to engage fully in our discussions.

Jodie had a slight physical disability in that she was hard of hearing, thus she frequently misheard conversations between friends. For this Jodie was ridiculed, also being called a baby because she mispronounced some words. Given that Jodie had attended play group and pre-school groups with the same girls that were now ridiculing her, I wondered when the upsetting behaviour had started. Jodie's mother thought her daughter and friends had played and mixed well together right through schooling years until the move into high school. It was then that the classes had become streamed on ability. The result being Jodie was not with her friends for most of the school day.

At school break times in secondary school, when Jodie had sought her peer group friends, they were not to be found in the usual meeting places. Jodie had come to dread break and lunch times because she was on her own. With her mother's advice, Jodie had started to frequent the school library during break in the school day, and one of the librarians had noticed what she described as a lonely child, sitting out of sight of the library entrance. The librarian had made contact with the school nurse, who had subsequently asked to see Jodie. Afterwards the nurse had telephoned Jodie's mother to share her concern about Jodie being upset and tearful without being able to explain why. Clearly there was a network of support at school, with adults who had Jodie's interests at heart. This is an important element that aids the recovery journey in cases where bullying is the presenting issue and this information was shared with Jodie's parents.

I divulged that I had knowledge of working with children who had experienced bullying behaviour, which led to Jodie's mother explaining that she, too, had been bullied at school. The consequences of this being that she found it hard to support Jodie in what she was experiencing at present. Jodie's anguished mother did not want to be seen as an over-protective parent and this had left her feeling powerless to help. although she clearly wanted to. Added to which, her own experience of bullying had made her hypersensitive to Jodie's plight. In fact I was beginning to gather that Jodie had found little of the resilience and strength she needed from her mother, and that this had left her feeling vulnerable.

The timing of this parental meeting was not ideal, since it

was mid-November and only a few weeks of therapy could be offered before the winter break. However, we reached the decision together that it was better not to delay the start date for therapy and arrangements were made to meet Jodie the following week.

Therapeutic Work

I was surprised when Jodie and I initially met for a short time for contracting and familiarisation with the room and resources. I had not expected to be working with an adolescent who presented as a very young child. However, as the work unfolded, I came to realise that Jodie saw herself as the baby in the family, being the youngest of three children and the only daughter.

As the first session got underway, Jodie shared how she had liked playing with her brothers when she was younger. She recalled a time when they had been 8 and 10, she being 4 years old, and how they had a part of the garden at home, that was just for them to play in. There they had created their own fun, making a den from tree branches and old blankets. Obviously Jodie was accustomed to playing outdoors, utilising what was available and being included in her brothers' and in the course of the games there appeared to be little exclusion, given her younger age and gender. I noted the theme of inclusion was surfacing early in our therapeutic work.

Whilst Jodie spoke of good memories from her younger years, I was aware of a mismatch between the rather adult young voice she was using and the young child's voice she had used at our first meeting to discuss the contract. As she talked, Jodie selected a basket of twigs and bark, and worked at building a small den from these items. It was a fine construction and I noted Jodie's level of manual dexterity was good, as was her problem-solving ability, since several times the twigs and bark had collapsed necessitating the need to restart the building project.

Her tale then spoke of the brothers leading their own lives now: the youngest one was in his last year at school and was hoping to take a gap year following his studies, perhaps to do some voluntary work abroad, whilst her eldest brother was now at university. In a disapproving tone Jodie told me the brother who was still at school had a girlfriend whom she sometimes liked but sometimes did not.

When writing my notes after the session, I realised Jodie was missing her brothers. They had been her first playmates who, it appeared, had included her naturally and without hesitation. Understandably the brothers were leading more independent lives, but Jodie was feeling left behind and left out. I began to see a link with the present-day situation Jodie was encountering at school.

In our second session Jodie returned to the theme of playing with her brothers in the garden at home, after she had noticed the kitchen toys stored in a transparent container. Whilst rummaging through them she asked to take them out and, with glee, held up two small pans for me to see. I asked what she was thinking about doing with them. 'I'm going to make mud pies in them.'

With this Jodie took some grey clay from the container, telling me she needed to mix some paint with the clay. She broke the grey clay into small pieces and put them into one of the pans. Next she poured water onto them and mixed it up into the clay with a stick. Green poster paint was stirred into the mixture, which by now was slopping over the side of the toy pan. Jodie told me the green was cabbage, which was good to eat but she did not really like it. Then roughly torn bits of red clay were added to the concoction. Jodie was in her element mixing up the mess, but now wanted some small stones as the final ingredient for her mud pies.

Fortunately, just outside the door to my office there was a small patch of gravel, so I joined Jodi in gathering a handful of irregularly shaped tiny pebbles. Jodie told me no one must see what we were doing and I assured her there was no one around in the grounds outside the office and that we were the only people in the room itself. Comforted, Jodie carried on the mud pie-making activity. To complete this concoction Jodie returned to rummaging amongst the kitchen toys to locate several coloured plates and, using a spatula, she slopped some of the concoction onto each. I could see her delight when playing, just as a pre-school child would, with the mess. And mess there was!

When the mud pie mixture had been slopped it was really slopped, and was now evident everywhere: on the floor, the table, Jodie and me. In fact, I was quite enjoying myself too and whilst I reminded myself to mention the need to keep the room safe, Jodie safe and me safe, my mind had engaged with this line of thinking too slowly! The slowness and the pleasure in our activity meant I needed to spend time after Jodie had left, clearing up everything carefully to ensure the room was back to its usual neat and tidy appearance. Fortunately Jodie had worn an overall that I kept for messy activities and my hands washed easily — my clothing had not been splattered.

Later, when completing records on the session, I recalled Jodie's need for the mess-making to remain unseen by the outside world. I softly hypothesised on the probability that Jodie's play might be a regression to happier times when she had fun creating and playing with others in a free way, and then I was overcome with sadness. It is hard for some children to have to grow up and leave their safe and protected lives when venturing into the academic world of prestigious educational establishments where the pressures and expectations placed upon them may seem heavy. I noted the sadness was not mine, but that I would hold it in awareness when next working with Jodie. Certainly our work was enabling Jodie's feelings to surface.

In her third session Jodie spoke of a recent family holiday during which her mother had spent time doing pictures of landscapes using oil pastels. Jodie had liked the pictures and had asked her mother to show her how to use oil pastels. So, whilst Jodie and her mother enjoyed time together making pictures, her brothers and father had gone sailing. Here I heard of a gender division within the family and wondered if this was the start of the older brothers beginning to separate from Jodie. Although Jodie had seemed not to notice this much at the time, because of her pleasure at the art-making activity with her mother.

She asked if she could use clay again and fashioned a lump of grey clay into a thickish hillock shape, then started making small boulder shapes that were used to build a dry stone wall. Apparently these walls had been seen during the holiday and they had watched someone repair a wall in which the stones had come away. Noteworthy was the theme of repairing something that was made from natural materials. Jodie busied herself with a fresh energy as she began making fields by scratching the hillock base with the rough edges of a large stone and a stick. She completed the model by adding a few sheep, exuding a sense of accomplishment as she put the few final details to the scene, which by now was looking quite artistic.

Jodie was certainly engaging well with the therapy, creating and processing with the clay in a way that informed me she was working through much that was not too far from the surface and thereby 'safe'. I considered this work was valuable in re-establishing a level of steadiness in Jodie before she was comfortable enough to bring her present worries with her peers into the sessions.

In our fourth session together, Jodie asked me to join her in making what resembled flying-saucer shapes in clay. When seven of these had been made, Jodie informed she intended making a cairn with them. She checked if I knew what a cairn was and I replied that it was a stone stack that historically had been built as a memorial. She listened with interest as I spoke and, although she gave no verbal response, a flicker of a smile passed her face. The cairn was made with care, with each stone being positioned so it would not topple the stack.

Jodie then told me it was springtime and made some tiny clay flowers, using both the grey and red clay. She was pleased with this clay creation, taking time to sit back and look at it from different angles, then turning it round to see if she approved of the sides that had been out of sight during the making process. The mention of springtime had not been lost on me, neither had the building of a clay sculpt that tells of ancestors.

During the next session, which was to be the last one before the winter holiday break Jodie made a contorted clay image in which a face could be seen. She groaned that it was ugly and grotesque and seemed unable to look at it; I wondered what she found in it that was difficult to face. Scooping up water in her hand, she threw it over the ugly clay image, whilst the other hand swished and squashed the clay, pulping it into an absolute mess. Snarling glimpses of anger flashed across Jodie's face; but then both hands were clapped together as she mischievously — and rather joyously — slid them up and down against each other, relishing the slippery clay. After this Jodie wanted to wash her hands to get rid of what she described as the 'dirt'. Again, I pondered on what dirt Jodie was washing away — what was she needing to get rid of?

In the cleaning up time right at the end of the session, Jodie seemed to lose a grip on our previous conversation, and she proceeded to tell of worries about her friendships at school. Here was an opportunity to discreetly enable an unfolding of her concerns and yet, as so often happens with adult clients, this opportunity was presented as the session was coming to a close. Now that we would be having a break of three weeks, I realised I was being left holding Jodie's inability to carry this unhappiness and the worry that she could not understood at a conscious level. She had unconsciously projected these concerns over to me to 'contain' until our session after the break.

Appreciating this is what therapy is all about, I reminded myself of the vital parental functions that Winnicott (1964) believed a therapist needed to fulfil: to soothe, affirm, validate and hold that which the infant is unable to handle for his or herself. Only when an infant has experienced these incredibly important aspects of parenting can the tiny person do this for self. When Jodie arrived for the first session after the break from therapy, it was noticeable how different she appeared. Looking relaxed and seeming more her age, she spent a good part of our time together sharing how much she had enjoyed the festive time over Christmas when her family were together. Her grand-mother's presence had been especially appreciated by Jodie, since she liked to hear stories of when her mother had been a young child and the family had then lived on a farm. It was a timely reminder of how important family connections and histories are offering 'anchoring' young people in providing a sense of belonging.

In recounting the minutiae of family life over the holidays, such as who drank coffee and who preferred tea, Jodie was letting me know that these things, although small, were significant. She had taken some clay, this time the red clay, and fashioned little shapes reminiscent of peanuts. I mirrored Jodie's actions in clay, while keeping my attention fixed on her, monitoring her facial expressions and attending to her narrative. When I looked down at what I had made, I thought the small shapes resembled human figures. I noticed Jodie's clay shapes also looked like people although with more definition than mine. When I mentioned that the session must end shortly, Jodie showed her annoyance, saying she was not ready to finish as she had not made all the people she needed: 'I haven't made all my family that are important to me.'

Now I knew we were moving into some deeper work and remembered the end of the session just prior to the break. Reassuring Jodie we could continue with the clay figures next week if they were wrapped up carefully, I could see this idea was not to her liking. She roughly seized my clay shapes, squashing them together with her clay people. I was a little taken aback at such an aggressive move.

When bringing the session records up to I date, I considered that Jodie was expressing some hurt. This seemed to be particularly so when I unintentionally thwarted her flow. Never-the-less, I knew this was an important aspect of her progress in developing ego strength, in that the aggressive impulse to squash the clay had been contained and not acted out on by the therapist.

It became clear in the next session that Jodie liked making

clay figures because she began talking about how she had enjoyed creating her family members in the previous week and what a pity it was that there had been insufficient time to complete her activities. I gently let Jodie know I had heard her disquiet about running out of time. Whilst sharing her views on the figure-making, she had moved across to the clay container, removed the lid, chose some clay and then began to work the lump almost without thinking.

Jodie asked me to sit close to her, because she was going to make some 'girls' from the clay and wanted me to help with the task; there was an air of reparation in her manner. Surprised and strangely delighted by the request, I positioned myself and waited and waited for instructions. What then transpired felt quite 'chummy.' As Jodie deftly fashioned two small clay girls, she asked if I knew how best to make clay clothes for them. I suggested a couple of ways, although Jodie seemed to appreciate the idea of rolling the clay out very thinly so she could cut out the clothing.

We sandwiched a thinnish slab of clay between two sheets of kitchen paper and carefully rolled over the 'sandwich' with a wooden rolling pin. In order to ensure the clay could be as thin as possible we gently peeled the top sheet of paper away from the clay. This was then replaced with a dry sheet, since the first stage of rolling had caused moisture from the clay to create tiny rips in the paper. Now we could continue rolling. Jodie was very satisfied with this experiment, especially when she took over the making of thin sheets of clay from me. Next she cut out clothing for the girls making tunic tops, shawls and jeans that she wrapped around them.

Once the clay girls were clothed, Jodie checked how much time was left of the session, telling me that it was very important to finish what she wanted to do in this seventh session. With a grin she told me the clay girls needed chairs to sit on. Only fifteen minutes were left, so we both took fresh lumps of clay and quickly hewed armchairs from them. With some fun in the air, we then placed the clay girls into the chairs, although of course some final adjustments were needed to get the girls sitting properly, by bending knees and re-positioning the bodies slightly.

'That's me and you,' Jodie laughingly shared, saying she wanted the models left unwrapped so they would dry out for the next session.

The Group of Girls

When Jodie arrived the following week it was clear she had been planning what to do in clay. Informing me she would be making some clay girls again, she described them this time as friends. I noted I was not required to sit near Jodie this time. Jodie showed how she was becoming adept at creating figures from clay; she made four girls with ease and, whilst engaged in the modelling, she asked me to roll some thin clay pieces so she could clothe the clay girls. This I duly did and was aware how Jodie looked across to my clay board to see how I was doing. I was a little curious about this, although I did not mention it. The four clay girls were different heights whereas the two clay girls from last week had been very similar sizes. Purposefully, and thoughtfully, Jodie set about clothing the clay girls. Now I understood that she had probably been assessing if I had rolled enough thin sheets of clay for the clothing activity.

Whilst clothing the clay girls Jodie had shared something about the character of each of them, naming them now as her peers. This was an extremely illuminating exercise, during which I became privy to Jodie's friendship group as she introduced them to me: she let me know who the most popular girl was, the quietest girl and which girl told sexual jokes. I did comment that Jodie had not made a clay girl to represent herself, but this seemed to fall on deaf ears. At the end of the session the four clay girls were placed into a box to dry out.

In session nine Jodie showed interest in the two clay girls seated in armchairs and the group of four clay girls described as friends. She lifted each model out of her box and positioned them on the large wooden board. Without speaking Jodie spent a few minutes looking at the dry clay figures.

'You are studying the clay figures carefully Jodie,' I commented. Jodie made no response. Instead she offered she would be making another clay girl this week. This figure turned out to be bigger than any of the previous ones, but no request came to make thin clay sheets for clothing. As Jodie made the figure, she spoke of some of her peers getting boyfriends. I listened and reflected where it felt appropriate, whilst also witnessing Jodie's sculpting of a nude female in which obvious attention to detail was dedicated to the creation of breasts.

'She's a tart, this girl,' Jodie said with disdain.

I subsequently heard the girl had strutted naked around the girls' changing room when the class had been changing for swimming lessons. I sensed I was not hearing the full story, rather, that Jodie was being selective in her account. Indeed, that is every client's prerogative and I did not push for information, as I could see Jodie was working through feelings that did not sit comfortably for her. I wondered whether her personal values had been challenged.

Indicating that she was intent upon continuing the clay figure modelling, Jodie began talking of two new friends she had made since rejoining the gymnastics after-school club. She told me she would make the friends in clay. As she started sculpting, I too, took some clay and created a clay figure, checking to make sure my figure was about the same size as Jodie's. In an animated fashion Jodie talked openly about the way the girls dressed and this lead to a conversation about the importance of image for adolescents. In essence it was a mature conversation, and I realised Jodie now seemed much more her age, as opposed to the seemingly young child of our first meeting.

The three clay figures were completed and Jodie wanted them clothed in appropriate gymnastic costumes. Together we rolled out thin sheets of clay, but it proved a tricky task to make the snug costumes fit the clay figures. Relaxed, Jodie covertly made reference to the adolescent girls' developing figures, particularly as she bent the figures into gymnastic poses.

I surmised that the intimidating behaviour that Jodie had experienced probably had a fair bit to do with puberty and sexuality, and since this notion had come into mind during the session it felt appropriate to voice my thinking. Jodie became serious as I openly talked of sexuality. She listened and responded to me, describing why she had found it hard to tell her parents and school staff what had been upsetting her. Intimate and personal concerns for pubescent youngsters can be agony to share with known adults.

Knowing this was our last session together before the parental meeting, we talked through what she wanted her parents to hear of our work. Jodie explained she wanted to describe her work to her mother; my role was to be a supporter and speak when Jodie included me. This indicated Jodie had found her voice and with it a level of confidence that did her justice. I felt proud of Jodie and admired her courage.

The meeting took place with Jodie, her mother and I present, and we experienced an honest and warm interchange. I was somewhat surprised when Jodie asked her mother if she could continue in therapy for another school term. This equated to another ten sessions. With her mother listening, I explored with Jodie the reasons she might have for wishing to continue the therapy throughout another term. She simply replied she liked working with me because it was helping her to feel stronger, and she still did not feel as strong as she wanted to feel. It was therefore agreed our work would carry on with a new contract to end after ten weeks. What was more surprising in our sessions together was that Jodie never worked with clay again. Instead she moved into collage and montage work, often with the theme of self-image.

When the final session arrived, Jodie chose to take home all her creations but what she left behind was my conclusion that the clay work from our earlier sessions had really served its purpose in getting right into the heart of Jodie's worries.

Discussion

Jodie belonged in a family where her upbringing could be described as good. By all accounts she did not suffer traumatic experiences that could have disturbed her development psychologically. However, because of Jodie's own mother's experience of being bullied when she was a child, she was unable to offer the emotional 'holding' and 'containment' of fear that Jodie needed — and I believe her mother subconsciously knew this.

A significant aspect of this case was that, in terms of Winnicottian theory, Jodie's father being 'unavailable' emotionally to support his wife in emotionally holding the family, and the help of an outside professional who *could* offer this was sought. A mother who feels emotionally stronger would usually be more robust in coping with her children's struggles. The therapist's ability to provide an emotional backbone is crucial to the efficacy of this kind of work. I liken this to the therapist's psyche acting almost as a surrogate psyche for the client, whilst the client's own ego starts to strengthen.

That said however, Jodie was a sensitive soul and sensitive children sometimes struggle to understand changes that naturally occur in all families, especially when the changes have not been openly discussed. As an adolescent subject to raging hormones, Jodie's equilibrium will have fluctuated considerably in any case. And family life itself ebbs and flows; the closeness and distance experienced in family relationships shifts naturally, finding a new balance only with time.

Given that Jodie's brothers had either left or were about to leave home, she had noticed an absence of companionship. Against this backdrop her worries at school surfaced and, since she was already struggling, she felt vulnerable. The severity of the bullying behaviour that Jodie experienced, is hard to determine. But its impact on her at that specific, vulnerable period in her adolescence meant that Jodie felt emotionally hurt, wounded and unprotected.

Chapter 13

Eating conditions:
Libby (age 14)

Reasons for Selecting this Case

I wish to share experiences concerning work with eating issues in therapy, and the case of Libby in particular. I also aim to demonstrate the application of the 'Theory of Contact' mentioned in Chapter 1, 'Clay Therapy: Theoretical Underpinning'. The reader will notice throughout the study the use of the 'five lenses' in order to clarify the process taking place and so aid further understanding of theoretical application. See also Appendix, 'Theory of Contact: Physical, Emotional, Spiritual and Metaphorical', for a more detailed account of this theoretical underpinning.

Introduction

Labelling children's and adolescent's complaints can be uncomfortable for some therapeutic practitioners, and because issues surrounding eating are usually incredibly complex, it seems preferable to refer to these as eating conditions as opposed to eating disorders.

A parent or carer with concerns about a child's eating worries usually channels a request for support through the medical route via a General Practitioner, who may then refer the child and family to a child and adolescent mental health team. However, waiting lists can be long and understandably adults around the child or the adolescent struggling with an eating concern become anxious at the inability to access help immediately.

Usually an eating difficulty has had the client in its grip for some time before parents realise there is a problem that needs to be addressed. This may happen for two reasons. Firstly, the client is usually good at hiding the eating situation from family members and parents who, whilst they may have an awareness of the problem, may also be fearful of what is often termed an eating 'disorder'. Secondly, sometimes a parent may have an awareness that there is a problem, but may feel quite disempowered to act on the knowledge.

How do we know, as parents or carers, when a faddy eating issue has become an eating condition necessitating outside help, especially when so many younger children will only eat beef burgers or fishfingers or Marmite soldiers? Eating conditions can be elusive of definition, when compared with other medical disorders — although this is not to say eating difficulties are necessarily medical disorders.

Returning to the idea that, at best, when medical intervention has been sought many parents have shared concerns that things are not happening fast enough for them, or that they are not seeing results. Such is the fear surrounding eating worries. This is when parents will often make contact requesting some therapeutic support in between CAMHS (Child and Adolescent Mental Health Services) visits. Since I am prepared to work within such a contract, I inform and seek out the opinion of other professionals involved to ensure that this arrangement is acceptable to them and complementary to the work they are undertaking with the client.

To date, the medical profession has been fully supportive of such arrangements. The key here is to ensure transparency and a multi-agency approach to the work in supporting the client and family as best as is possible. It is unusual for other professionals to decline. There are a variety of reasons for this, but perhaps professional practitioners generally feel that no one intervention is better than another in attempting to work with an eating condition. Maybe medicalisation of an eating concern does not always take into account the broader and fuller family story. In some cases a clinical approach, has been described as lacking in warmth, since the physical surrounding are viewed as emotionally cold by the family. These are some of the reasons given by young people who no longer wish to attend clinics.

Case Background Information

Libby was informed that, due to long waiting lists for medical interventions for clients presenting with eating concerns, a first appointment might take at least six months to come through. Libby was therefore referred to my practice by the pastoral deputy headteacher at the local secondary school she attended. My contract with Libby was a holding one, with agreement to only eight sessions, due to an impending holiday the family had arranged, but I was prepared to work with Libby knowing all adults concerned with the case understood this was to be an interim intervention. Clearly there was an underlying complex eating condition that required medical help and which could be worked with once the CAMHS appointment was scheduled.

Therapeutic Work

On first meeting with Libby I wondered how easily she would engage, as I had been informed she was a reluctant talker. There was a hesitancy about Libby; she presented as quite reserved and sullen and did not seem to warm to the session. Strangely I felt nervous, I reassured myself the contract was for eight sessions and that I need not put myself under pressure. Then I considered where this pressure was coming from. Was it of my own making? I had been clear about what I could offer, but nevertheless had understood that once Libby was my client our therapeutic relationship would be the focus for all the worries and hopes of the adults surrounding this young woman.

I wondered if the school felt relief at having handed the problem of Libby on to me — or did Libby's parents hope that my work with Libby would solve the eating worries, thereby enabling cancellation of medical intervention? These concerns are concerns I have often heard supervisees voicing. No matter how experienced practitioners are, if we are working with freshness of insight (Casement, 1985) we still experience others' projections, hopes and expectations and — I would go as far as to say — when we stop feeling these, we should stop working as a therapist!

Our ability to feel and get in touch with strong emotion is at the core of the work, but here we need to monitor transference and counter-transference components. The two are different sides of the same coin. Clinical supervision helps to unravel what belongs to us and what belongs elsewhere. Knowing my pre-disposition to take responsibility for others, I must work with finely attuned antennae in order to monitor this. It was clear to me that my tendency to take responsibility was active in the first encounter with Libby: I could almost feel the need of others' need that I solve Libby's predicament.

Clients presenting with eating conditions are usually very self-controlling, not only with eating, but also in speech and emotions. Rather therefore, than initiating too much talking therapy, I moved into using montage as a starting activity in the hope of beginning to build a relationship with Libby. Montage (not to be confused with collage, which is the use of a variety of mediums to create an image or process) is where images, pictures and words are cut or torn from magazines, then juxtaposed to create a new composition. It is important to ensure that a varied selection of magazines is available that are neither gender nor subject specific.

Libby unenthusiastically nudged magazines around. In the face of diffidence it can be hard to remember the old saying 'trust the process'. Yet while it is the therapists function to hold the hope that something can be worked with, there are times when this can be elusive — apathy is powerfully negative. With a little more effort Libby stretched an arm further, suggesting that she was becoming marginally more interested. Gingerly, she pulled a birding magazine towards her. Slowly turning the pages she asked if I was a bird watcher. I shook my head saying that although I like birds I have trouble seeing birds as some are so small. No response ensued from Libby. Nevertheless, I consciously stored in the recesses of my mind that Libby had selected a bird magazine and was curious about me and birds.

In a first session with a new client I am mindful that the information presented often holds the essence or kernel of the emotional work that requires attention for a feeling of wellbeing to eventually be achieved. Reaching for the scissors Libby focused her attention on cutting out pictures of small birds. I thought she was about to cut round each individual bird but that did not happen. Instead a shadow of the birds was left round the image, making it hard to tell what the background had been. In an attempt to build a working relationship with Libby, I asked if she knew what birds she had selected. There was a cool interchange when naming the birds, but I was being kept at a distance.

Since I usually enjoy warm relationships with clients, I was mindful of the distance, again considering this as a significant aspect to our work. By now I was beginning to sit back in the chair to give Libby the space she seemed to need. Libby then asked what I wanted her to do with the birds. As the end of the session was in sight, I offered that the cut-out pictures could be used the following week if she wanted and that in the meantime they could be kept safe in an envelope. It is hard to imagine what I've just described as taking up a fifty-minute session and yet it did, such was the slow pace of the session. Later, when writing notes, I recorded that this client would need some space in the working relationship and that it was imperative I worked at Libby's pace, even though the contract was a short one and that somehow I felt outside pressure to 'make Libby's eating worries better'.

Session two showed a mild shift in Libby's view of coming to therapy, whereby the sullen countenance parted to offer a slight smile of recognition when we greeted each other. I had laid out the cut-out birds from the first session, in a fan shape, so that they appeared to be coming out of the envelope — mainly because I wanted them to be visible and tempting, should Libby decide to take the bird theme up again. Perhaps I was also aware that when a client's story begins to unfold there is a sense of something attempting to emerge. Attempting to put myself into Libby's experience, I felt there needed to be a half-hidden half-open invitation to work with the birds.

When facilitating training workshops, I am asked how I know what I need to do in a particular session. My only reply to this type of enquiry is that I am guided by intuition. I soon know if I have not understood, misjudged or simply just 'didn't get' it because a client will ignore or moves off to a different activity, as if what I have just said or done is of no consequence. That said, there are always exceptions where perhaps I really 'got it, but the timing was not right, perhaps due to the length or depth of the therapeutic relationship — or possibly to the fact that something was being acted out in the relationship.

'The birds are here from last week,' I commented casually.

'So they are.' Libby replied.

I wondered if I had caught a hint of haughtiness which sometimes may mask hurt. I did not overlook this, possibly significant, interchange between us, but stored it away, thinking it may inform our work later.

Libby seemed to assume that montage-making would continue in this second session, because she looked straight at the magazines. This week she rifled through the pile in a more determined fashion, pushing aside the more stylish or girlie magazines favouring countryside brochures. Next she cut out half-page sections of landscapes. Libby laid down a sheet of buff-coloured sugar paper and began arranging the landscape pictures so they overlapped. These were then stuck down. Afterwards she took a great deal of care to position the small pictures of the birds correctly. When satisfied with the layout, she glued them down on top of the landscapes.

During the montage-making we talked about Libby's love of nature and her tenderness and feelings towards animals and living things. I was amazed at this youngster who held views in line with Buddhist philosophy and I sat with this, delighting in the way she was describing her sensitivity to the natural world. 'And this is therapy?' I asked myself, when I acknowledged how enjoyable working with this client was turning out to be. Much eye contact was now taking place between us and I realised we were building a therapeutic relationship with a sense of trust being mutually experienced. The empathic attunement was aligning each with the other.

At the start of session three Libby seemed less inhibited. She entered the therapy room with more of a presence and I wondered if, since the previous session seemed to have been enjoyed by both, a relationship bond was becoming established. On the table between us was the countryside montage. Libby studied it for a little while then told me how birds are free to fly where they like and that they can see from above and look down on what is happening.

I considered Libby's idea, responding that, yes, birds have an overview — what we call a 'birds' eye view'. Wondering where this narrative was heading I told myself to go gently, stay unhurried; my intuition was advising that this was essential. Libby's eyes moved to the other side of the therapy room and she hesitantly asked if she could use the clay.

'You'd like to use clay,' I stated.

I took a large wooden board propped up against the wall and Libby placed it on the floor. Libby's manner seemed very decisive — there seemed to be a new energy in the room. She then seated herself on the floor and began by asking what she should make.

'How about trying an organic, free flowing activity.'
These words appeared to appeal to Libby, as she smiled.

'Okay.'
I suggested perhaps Libby and I could work on individual pieces of clay simultaneously in a spirit of playing in the presence of each other. This way we could play in the presence of each other but not essentially together, just as small children do when close by to a trusting adult.

As we worked with the clay on the floor, our bodies would also move, and I was mindful that the movements of our diaphragm in the act of breathing helps our inner organs to receive something of a massage. Once we begin to breathe slowly, using the diaphragm, this has a positive effect on the therapeutic work, 'freeing' us to go deeper. Overall, we would experience a rhythm between body, breathing and activity, enabling a connection with the unconscious — and introducing the possibility that simple intangible 'essences' within us might actually take visible form.

Libby worked with a smallish, hand-sized lump of clay and started to form a sphere shape, using the heels of her hands. With thumb and finger movements she gently teased the clay out to create what almost looked like fish fins on either side of the sphere. This took some time, maybe five minutes or so. (This stage is Lens 1 in the Theory of Contact; see diagram and text in Chapter 1, 'Clay Therapy: Theoretical Underpinning of Clay Theory'.)

At the same time as creating the 'fish fins', she continued to work on different facets of the original sphere; I thought I could see details resembling bird feathers. Whilst Libby was modelling, I worked with a smaller lump. I realised I had been working slowly, stroking my clay, yet almost mirroring Libby's movements. Stroking movements always bring to mind soothing feelings and I felt relaxed and quietened, wondering if the same was happening for Libby. In the activity of working with separate clay forms simultaneously, there is a sense of accompanying the creation of something that often becomes significant. In other words, a 'co-creation': together yet, separate. (Lens 2, Theory of Contact).

I was aware at this point in the session we were beginning to enter a deeper phase of the work, in which an inter-connectedness between us would continue (Lens 3, Theory of Contact). This is a crucial time and so I monitored my interjections most carefully. This state of flux is alive to possibilities and potential, and unrecognised thoughts and ideas may surface possibly illuminating new meaning and understanding.

Tentatively and quietly I wondered out loud what might be

forming. Almost whispering, Libby said, 'A bird.' There was some eye contact between us, but since this is a critical stage in the clay work, rather than responding verbally I nodded my acknowledgement. I know these slight gestures are registered by clients, therefore I always refrain from verbal interjection until I feel it is appropriate to speak. It is as if we break the spellbound reverie if words are uttered for the sake of it. Through the 'holding' by the therapist, the work can move seamlessly into the beginning of the story that needs to unfold. (Lens 4)

Clay Bird

Having acknowledged that a bird was being created, I mentioned remembering the cut-out birds from the first session. This comment was offered almost as if it was a discovery, which of course it was. In all our work, if we remain freshly attuned in our contemplations with the client we know then we are following the client authentically. Now the therapeutic relationship felt as if it were a more trusting one as we moved deeper into the clay work and, since we were mutually accepting of each other's presence, I pushed tentatively asking what the bird might need.

'Wants to fly away.'

'Fly away.' I reflected.

'Yes fly away from places it doesn't like; like when it doesn't want to see, or something that disturbs it'.

We were beginning to work through metaphor. The fact that the bird was no-gender cautioned me not to probe too deeply, after all this was only the third session.

'So this bird has seen something that has perhaps caused it to be upset.'

Libby gently nodded.

Here I knew we were moving into a deeper level of conscious-ness. This is when it is paramount to watch and track carefully. Nothing should be assumed; I was taking my cues from the client and staying with using the client's words.

'Yes, bird was terrified.'

I empathised with the bird.

'Poor bird, how awful feeling terrified.'

There was stillness in the room. The quietness between us was palpable. I was aware I was holding my breath, almost in readiness — for what, I did not know. When reflecting on the session later, I was quite amazed that in just two sessions we had established a relationship and plumbed to considerable depth. When this happens, we know the client is ready to do the work, but a client's defences are there for a good reason. They are there for emotional safety and experience tells me that the client will let down their defences when they are ready too, and only then.

On a number of occasions adult clients have said, 'I want you to make me go deeper — I think I should.'

'Okay, go deeper then, tell me more,' I reply.

By gently, metaphorically 'holding' the client, they are enabled to move in readiness to go deeper. For they will when the time is right. Perhaps they are intimating they are ready to let down their defences, but checking that I am available to emotionally 'hold' that which will come forward. The younger the children, the closer they are to feeling their emotions, therefore they surface much more quickly. An adolescent with an air of sophistication requires a different approach.

'Bird', had been carefully placed in a small, high-sided plastic container and the clay and container were wrapped in polythene to make everything airtight. Libby had not been sure what she wanted to do with Bird and this informed the symbolic manifestation of Libby's bird was still alive to her senses and unconscious, meaning the creation's energy was still potent.

During session four I had incorrectly assumed we would work on the clay bird. Just when the therapist thinks she might know where we may be going with the work, things get blown off course. This change of course, is always client-motivated, since it is the client who takes the work where it needs to go. For me it was a salutary reminder to remain open and alert to the newness of each session. Libby used the session to tell her concerns over schoolwork, as she was in the year for taking examinations.

Eating conditions may often accompany pressure over exam successes and academia, but so far in our work there had been no mention by Libby of her eating worries. Towards the end of the session I enquired of Libby what needed to happen (if anything) with the clay bird, for I wondered if I was picking up a sense of the bird's energy; it was almost as if there were an entity in the room of which we were not speaking. She then requested to see her creation from the previous week and asked me to check if it was still damp enough to work with the following week. Together we touched the bird and mutually agreed it would be damp enough to continue with it next week. if Libby chose to do so.

Interestingly session five was given over to talk about a small group of peers with whom Libby was acting in a forthcoming music performance. Libby's feelings were explored round this event and again I wondered what might be happening in the work between us, since this was what I call 'everyday workings'.

Whilst in therapy sessions we can help a client to make some sense of situations and to come to understand what relationships mean, there nevertheless appeared to be some avoidance of what I felt might be troubling Libby further.

However, I realised the session had been worthwhile because it provided an opportunity for Libby to learn more about herself and this is a natural progression of adolescent identity development. And then, just as the session drew to a close, Libby announced with some urgency that she needed to check the clay bird again to ensure it had not dried.

In the following session, without any prompting, Libby quickly took up telling of a story that had clearly disturbed her. A couple of months previously she had been walking home from school when she overheard a group of younger boys, who she did not know, talk of drowning a cat in the stream close to the school. I could well imagine that this episode had had on sensitive, nature-loving Libby and was quick to empathise. Apparently she had not been noticed by the boys, but she had heard their cruel laughter.

'You heard and you hurried on your way home knowing there was nothing you could do.'

'Yes, that's right, I couldn't do anything. I couldn't even tell anyone about it. because I didn't know if it really was true and, if it was, I couldn't believe anyone would be so cruel.' Libby bleated despairingly.

I thought for what seemed some time as I 'held' the quietness.

Then I said, 'I was thinking how it is that birds see and hear and they can fly away.'

'Oh yes.' Libby said in a sad tone.

I wondered at this point if I had been too hasty with introducing the idea of birds hearing and seeing, since it was obvious that the clay bird was not in Libby's consciousness at that point and yet I was still 'holding' the bird's energy. Libby had not seen the link between the making of her clay bird and the narrative that had just been relayed, but I thought it was worth taking the risk of voicing my thoughts. On consideration I felt the relationship was firmly established enough to make this attuned response positive and I had carefully checked to ensure I was not working from a counter-transference perspective.

Taking the clay bird (which was now leather-hard in that it held its shape well without easily being squashed or damaged, but still moist enough to work with), Libby almost caressed it. I remembered how I had stroked and smoothed my clay form in session three when Libby made the bird. Here there had been some mirroring of movement, which lets us know that the therapist's mirror neurons are responding and attuned to that which they are witnessing. These moments, when time feels suspended in the session, can seem almost 'otherworldly'; there is a felt phenomenon that can only be described as spiritual, a moment in which something sacred and profound is being experienced.

When it felt appropriate, I spoke of the bird being able to get away, and the way in which Libby herself had done just that, after she heard the boys boasting of what they had done to the cat; but the memory was not a good one for her. It was a fearful one. I then went on to tell her how I would have been very, very, upset if I had experienced what Libby had experienced and how, I, too, probably wouldn't have known what to do. I added that I also would have wondered if I should have told someone about these boys and what they had done, but probably would have been too frightened of the consequences, I think. There was a long quietness. Libby seemed to be thinking about what I had shared.

Libby then ventured further, sharing how the awfulness of what the boys had done to the cat had meant she never wanted to hear of an animal ever being harmed again. Libby certainly was a sensitive soul and the death of the cat had made her turn to eating a vegetarian diet. Often after horrible experiences our thoughts change and we feel differently. I responded with a reflection that sometimes, when we are powerless to do very little this can leave us with a sense of shame.

This seemed to hit a note for Libby for she said, 'Yeah, I

haven't liked myself for not doing something.'

Strangely, the little clay bird had accomplished its work. It had been created by Libby, metaphorically used (in essence) to free Libby of the burdensome memory of helplessly listening to awful details of a poor cat's death, and then had provided her with a new understanding of what the experience meant for her. (Lens 5)

Libby did not attend session seven due to illness. I wondered if perhaps the previous session had been especially poignant for her?

In the following session Libby appeared less fragile. I enquired about the illness that had prevented her attending session seven, but had the sense I was being brushed off with her saying she felt better. Before the session I had opened the container in which the clay bird had been kept safely and left it on the table for Libby to see. Libby noticed it immediately, so I asked what needed to happen to bird. Libby thought for a while, then asked for it to be photographed for her ready for next week. She suggested she could cut the image of the bird out of the photograph and stick her own clay bird on her countryside montage. Libby told me that she would like to think of the clay bird 'going back to nature' and that perhaps we could bury it outside,

I dutifully photographed the bird and with reverence, Libby chose a final resting place in the garden adjacent to the office. The resting place was unbelievably close to where my cat had been buried some years before Libby had come to work with me, though Libby was unaware of this fact. Gently, Libby placed the bird half into the soil and then took a large water lily floating close to the edge of the pond and laid this over the bird. It was a profound and moving experience that we shared. Suffice is to say, the psyche knows what it needs.

Discussion

I do not know what happened to Libby, I cannot say if her eating condition changed. My work was that of a holding contract, in the course of which I would accompany Libby on a physical and visual exploration of an experience that had disturbed her enough to change her eating pattern and cause worry to her family.

In conclusion, we can never be certain what deeper issues are waiting to be worked with, but if we are ready and prepared to work through the client's story with them, the core of the concern may be located upon. When we work at some depth we can never underestimate the potency of the journey together. It is hard to put into words the feelings that arise when we know we have connected with another at a spiritual level.

Chapter 14

Shame and Sexual Matters:
Dylan (age 15)

Reasons for Selecting this Case

The case material written on Dylan is included to show how there are times in clay therapy when it is appropriate to remain working through metaphor. This means understanding issues brought to therapy that are not absolutely translated, not literal. Rather, when a client is relaxed within the environment and with the therapeutic practitioner, an understanding is reached, working imaginatively with the clay creations or processes.

A secondary reason for writing up the work of Dylan is to illustrate the way in which it is possible to do further, brief therapeutic work after a year or more, almost as a top-up intervention.

Introduction

Adolescent years can be fraught with difficulties associated with sexuality. This phase of physical growth and human development is notoriously emotionally turbulent. The fact that adolescents are increasingly referred for therapeutic support and guidance is therefore not surprising. Progress and success with this age group is difficult to chart, because the adolescent client is constantly changing and evolving with their struggle to find a sense of equilibrium in the midst of this occupies a great deal of their 'thinking space'.

Case Background

Dylan's family had been at the centre of investigations carried out by a multi-agency team of professionals when his younger sister's primary school teacher had raised concerns upon hearing what was happening within the home. Meetings had been held and, whilst there were no safeguarding children issues uncovered, Dylan's family was allocated a key worker to support individual members when his parents separated. The key worker had been responsive to Dylan's request to meet with a counsellor, so Dylan and I had met weekly for 23 sessions in a school art room where we were free to use the various creative mediums available. He was 13 at the time.

Two years later, a pastoral leader from the school Dylan attended, approached me with a view to seeing Dylan again. A very brief contract of four weeks was negotiated with Dylan, because he was due to start a work experience placement, which negated a longer contract.

Therapeutic Work

I was pleased to see Dylan again. Whilst he had grown much taller, he was still of slight build so when his shoulders drooped he looked gangly. Apparently Dylan had asked to meet with his previous counsellor because she would know something about his background already. He told me this himself saying he would be embarrassed to tell his story to another person just yet.

This second phase of therapy took place in my private practice office where there is clay, sand and the arts mediums readily available. Dylan reminded me how we used to work with the paints and charcoal and these were offered again, but he was more interested in using clay.

Holding a lump of clay over a wooden board, Dylan talked quietly about the difficulties he was experiencing at home. As he spoke I noticed he was pulling bits of clay from the main lump in an agitated manner. He said he was finding it hard to say what he really wanted to talk about. This anguished young man required time and I was not going to hurry the conversation in any way. I reassured Dylan that he was to take his time and just to let his hands tell the story with the clay.

He seemed to like this idea. I went on to say that I thought clay would help him to express what he needed to express — and when he was ready to express it. The atmosphere in the room was hushed, just the noise of the clock ticking and the gentle thuds when Dylan dropped bits of clay onto the board. Staying with what the client clearly needs is a privilege, for it nearly always brings forth that which is requiring attention.

Within a few minutes I became aware of Dylan's more deliberate actions, as the aimless pulling away and dropping of bits of clay had turned into a determined targeting of the board. I silently ruminated on Dylan's movements: his initial 'pulling things to pieces' had rapidly turned into an angrier activity. Could this mean he was showing he felt himself 'in pieces', I wondered?

As the clock ticked on and the thudding of the clay grew stronger, Dylan spoke of being in a local supermarket, when he had accompanied his father to buy groceries. Suddenly his father had veered towards the ladies clothing and underwear section. Dylan described himself as being mortified when he saw two girls from his school in the next shopping isle. Just as the girls rounded the corner, they saw Dylan's father holding a pair of women's briefs against himself, checking for size. Dylan said he swivelled on the spot to face the opposite direction, pretending not to see the girls as they curled up sniggering, nudging and pushing each other away and out of sight. Dylan did not know the girls by name, but nevertheless he thought they would know of him.

After the shopping trip and in the car on the way home to his father's new flat, Dylan's father had commented on his quietness. Dylan shared with me that he had not wanted to respond to his father for fear of blurting something out that he may later regret having said but that he felt so confused. I heard that Dylan felt his father was very mixed up; he knew his father had been on the internet to search out sites giving information on cross-dressing. Dylan spat out the word, "filth, absolute, filth."

For this 15-year-old male the idea of his father cross-dressing within the family home was completely unacceptable, and he was relieved his father now lived elsewhere. Appreciating this was a delicate subject for Dylan, I realised that it was paramount to proceed with heightened sensitivity. I felt Dylan's hurt and emotional pain. This was not my pain, but Dylan's. I was experiencing Dylan's pain as if it was my own, therefore acting as a 'container' for the feelings which were split off and un-bearable for him. (Bion, 1970)

Knowing the session could veer into an exploration of Dylan's thoughts about his father, which, of course would be useful, it was nevertheless important to bring the focus back to how Dylan was feeling and what all this meant for him. Perhaps it was because I remembered we only had four sessions together that I felt time was of the essence? But each time I attempted to change the focus I was thwarted, thus realising the time was not right for Dylan.

I was being too hasty! After all, Dylan's energy was likely to have been spent in the session owing to the trouble he had experienced in beginning to talk about his difficult feelings con-cerning his father's behaviour. Whilst therapeutic practitioners may be familiar with talking through difficult aspects of being human, it is worthwhile remembering for clients, particularly adolescents, this can be excruciatingly painful.

Dylan arrived five minutes early for session two. I took this as a signal that he was either anxious about being late or keen to start the work. Either way, the meaning is possibly similar. I did not explore this with Dylan as I might have with an adult client because I was certain the content of the session was likely to be enough to contend with. It is productive to consider when and why a therapist does something in or around a session with a specific client that is 'out of the norm' for, while one is considering this, subconscious information about the work often surfaces.

His head still drooping, which gave him the appearance of having the troubles of the world on his shoulders, Dylan settled himself into a chair and rearranged the cushions to make himself comfortable. He almost seemed to be creating a nest for himself, as if he needed somewhere safe and in my office he was free from the prying outside world.

'Comfy?' I asked. "

'Yeah,' He smiled back.

I then shuffled the cushions around in my chair. Dylan's head lifted as he watched me.

'That's better,' I said as I settled myself. We were both ready to start.

He told me that during the week he had been thinking over our first session and went on to talk of his feelings towards his father. Perhaps my prompting of this towards the end of the first session had sown seed. Dylan shared that he was disappointed with his father, who he felt had embarrassed him in the shop when handling the women's briefs against himself. He thought his father weak, not manly, and in Dylan's eyes this diminished both his own and that of his father's maleness. He felt cheated of not having a 'macho Dad'.

He claimed his father had let his family down and could not understand how he dared to do this to Dylan's mother. Dylan could see his mother was suffering and struggling. Whilst he said he still loved his father, he hated what his father's behaviour was doing to his mother. For that, he was angry. He questioned why his father was not out at football matches like other fathers, or doing something like fishing which he identified as a man's sport. The present moment did not appear to be the right time to consider if there could be found a balanced perspective of his father; It was important to stay with Dylan's line of thought.

Next followed a discussion on what Dylan thought of as 'manly', and in our explorations of the subject he showed his willingness to consider different perspectives. This led me to consider that perhaps there was something else bothering Dylan that so far, had not come to light. I reflected back to Dylan his varied perspectives on maleness, mentioning that I felt there was possibly more to his thinking than appeared on the surface. I felt able to push a little further, because there already existed an established, trusting therapeutic relationship; I would not have done this had the session only been the second of a new contract. Dylan was prepared to consider the gentle challenge I posed. Quietness settled on the room. Again, honouring the thinking time Dylan seemed to need, I waited. Dylan spoke of the humiliation he felt when his father's behaviour had been seen by two of his female peers from his school. He was furious that he had been seen with his father. This was far worse for Dylan, it appeared, than the actual cross-dressing his father was engaged in. Exploring a little further, Dylan was able to identify just how shaming this public exposure had been. Although he said he would prefer it if his father were not to cross-dress at all, he was mainly concerned that his peers should not know of it.

At this stage in the session Dylan seized some clay and began pulling pieces off just as he had done in the previous week. Now he proceeded to throw them with vigour into a pile on the board. Next he pulled the pile from the board and squashed the lump, using both his hands. Much energy was expended in squashing, thumping and screwing up the clay. The clay was taking the full force of Dylan's surfacing anger and that is what is so beneficial when working with clay — it absorbs the given energy.

At the end of the session Dylan put the board on the floor and slammed down on the clay with his fists as hard as he could; then he trod on it, squashing it to a pulp. No words were necessary as I witnessed this strong emotion coming through. Later, I reflected that it is hard for a mild and gentle person to let out anger, yet Dylan had managed to do this in a manner that was appropriate and acceptable, in the safety of the office.

Yet again Dylan started to pull pieces off a lump of clay at the start of session three. However, this time when the clay lump had been fully pulled apart, I was surprised that Dylan began to scoop the pieces up, and cup them in one hand. This action seemed quite different to the previous two weeks. It was as if he was holding all the pieces, not dropping any;

they all mattered. Then, using both hands he pressed the pieces together, not aggressively, but yet with a particular strength in his movements.

I remained quiet as this work took place, mainly because I was unsure what was happening, although I was aware that I was 'containing' the process. When a series of actions seems to turn into a sequence, this is evidence that the psyche is on the move and therefore it is imperative the therapist remains fully attuned to what is unfolding. Gradually the clay began to be shaped as a totem form whose phallic reference was not lost on me, although Dylan informed me it was the stump of a tree.

Dylan's Tree

I attempted to interject, asking Dylan to tell me why the stump had taken this particular form: had a storm torn the rest of the trunk away or had the tree been cut down? Clearly I was being too specific in my questions — and certainly off-beam — because I received an emphatic, 'No!' However, Dylan did share that the tree had just stopped growing — but that it was its time to grow again. I accepted Dylan's narrative for he was the maker.

Painstakingly, Dylan made a tree with a tender young trunk topped by just a few spindly branches. The trunk did not look especially sturdy, but nevertheless it was a tree that was not collapsing under the weight of the clay branches. Dylan did express some concern that the tree may fall over, as it looked a little unbalanced. To remedy the situation he made a clay base that he called 'land', on which he cemented his tree, although he made no mention of roots. Now there was the earth, the trunk and the branches. Dylan was pleased with his efforts and admired what had been created in this third session. He requested I should keep the tree safe, so he could look at it the next session.

The symbolic meaning attached to trees filled my mind when writing my notes after the session: the notion of a vast tree spreading its branches throughout our cosmos — and perhaps the idea that a tree's roots inhabit our earthly underworld, while its branches reach for the heavens. Possibly Dylan's tree could be likened to an emotional backbone, which in turn supports emotional existence through the body. Some may infer this could be the temple of his soul.

The final of the four sessions arrived. Dylan entered the office with a more up-beat air about him and I learned that the visit to his work-experience placement earlier in the week had been an enjoyable one. He spent a few minutes admiring the clay tree made in the previous session, turning it round on the board and looking at it from different angles. Picking the tree up in his left hand Dylan, began trailing a finger across each of the spindly branches. The mood in the room was gentle. It seemed almost as if Dylan was caressing the branches. When clay creations are handled delicately, it can suggest the client is being caring and gentle with himself. This was a heart-warming scene.

Dylan placed the tree carefully on the board and stretched across to the clay container. He selected a lump of clay, which he then began to pat into a spherical form. As he rolled the sphere in between his cupped hands, I sensed his thoughts were somewhere else, for his breathing had slowed and it was as if he was calming himself with the repetitive action. I sat quietly appreciating the intimate moments that silence often brings in a session with a client.

Blinking, Dylan brought his attention back to the moment, looked at me, and started to talk about the animal rescue centre which was to be his work experience. He told me how cruel some people could be to animals. He thought he might get upset at seeing hurt and abandoned animals that had been pets at one time, but that it was very important there were people in the world who wanted to make a difference.

As this was the last session I was in a slight dilemma as to whether or not to attempt making links or associations between hurt animals and Dylan's hurt feelings. Whenever one is uncertain if something should be voiced in a therapy session, this is usually a sign it is better to leave it unsaid. I decided to trust that Dylan was finding his own way through the metaphors in his narrative.

Strangely, as these thoughts were going through my mind, Dylan started to toss the clay sphere from one hand to the other. His movements were mirroring my thinking; just amazing, such was the rapport between us that an unconscious communication was taking place, or so it seemed.

With one final throw of the clay sphere high into the air, Dylan caught it and put it right back in the clay container. The action was almost like a full stop to the work. A swift closing gesture before he picked up the clay tree that he wished to take away with him.

My work was done for this phase in Dylan's life. My compassion for his situation turned into admiration for a young chap who needed to find a path through his difficult family circumstances and I wished him well as he left.

Discussion

Dylan had been through a tough time. Whilst he could just about manage his feeling around his father cross-dressing, he had no wish for his family to be publically rumbled, because it made him feel seedy and ashamed. Shame is a crippling emotion that is caustic on the soul and corrodes levels of self-worth. What is more, shame rots the core of a person, preventing them from having a good perspective on themselves with self-criticism being a close relative to the feeling of shame.

I had worked with compassion in the first phase of therapy and still felt the same towards Dylan, which made me wonder if possibly Dylan, throughout his life, would need experiences of 'compassion injections' from time to time. In my attention to his latest difficulty, I had offered Dylan considered 'containment' for his level of distress which had certainly been reduced. Perhaps this was not totally as a result of the brief therapeutic intervention, but I felt with some certainty that it had contributed substantially.

Chapter 15

Depression and Family Relocation: Raz (age 16)

Reasons for Selecting this Case

The main reason for writing about the work with Raz is to illustrate the way so many adolescents experience sadness and melancholic periods when faced with changes outside of their control during this natural maturation processes. This case has also been selected to show when the therapeutic work undertaken is with a client whose early home life has been 'good enough' (Winnicott, 1964), the number of therapy sessions is likely to afford a shorter contract.

Introduction

The hormonal life of an adolescent is one of peaks and troughs. The adolescent is constantly having to adjust. Achieving balance and perspective in peer relations, social standing, cultural and gender identity and body image are all struggles that happen within a family context, whatever that may be for each individual youngster. Hence, it can be somewhat difficult to specify with absolute certainty when an adolescent is in a depressed state or merely experiencing a 'low' mood. Indeed some of these low moods can continue for a good length of time.

That said, changing family circumstances and dynamics often propel adolescents into finding themselves in positions or places where they have had no choice, thereby rendering them powerless and impotent. They may protest loudly and get noticed or become de-motivated and depressed, presenting as withdrawn and isolated.

Case Background Information

A caring class tutor at Raz's secondary school became concerned over how quiet the new 16-year-old male student seemed. Given that Raz had moved from an urban London home to a rural town in East Anglia, his reserve was probably not out of the ordinary, since the geographical-culture shift was huge. However, it was clear the teacher had picked up reasons for a deeper concern for Raz.

Raz's mother was of Ghanaian origin and his father was white British. When living in London, Raz's peers had been mainly of mixed race. He had been a street-wise adolescent, used to getting round on local buses to frequent cinemas or ten-pin bowling alleys. Raz's father had been offered a new job necessitating the family move. The move to a fenland town meant Raz had found himself living in a reasonably rural community in which life for him had become quiet, to the point of dullness.

When I first met Raz, he shared he did not fit in with the new setting and how his outlook was quite bleak. He expressed a strong wish to return to his former London area and was in constant contact with his previous friends via texting. Raz knew he would be leaving school in less than half a year and was impatient to go to college in London where he hoped to study information technology.

The difficult side of this desire was he knew he would be leaving behind his parents, with whom he had a reasonable relationship, as well as his sister who was two years younger than him, and towards whom he felt protective, since she was diabetic. We agreed to work for a few weeks, then review progress to help Raz with the transitioning phase he was struggling with, but also (as it turned out) to help him through the 'moving on' stage every adolescent experiences when they begin to wonder if it is time to leave home.

Therapeutic Work

In our first session together Raz identified how angry he was at not having a say over whether the family moved or not. But he was especially annoyed at the move taking place in October just before his mock examinations. He explained that he had done very little revision and as a consequence his mock examination results were low. I experienced Raz as a reasonably conscientious young person who previously had been confident in his abilities to meet the world head-on, but now felt uprooted and isolated. We initially explored what he thought he had lost through the relocation and both of us struggled to identify many gains.

Whilst he was aware that I offered creative therapy working through clay, Raz was very vocal during the first two sessions and clearly wanted to give full and rapid vent to his feelings out loud. It did not seem appropriate to invite involvement with clay, such was the need to allow time for his verbal expression.

Noting and commenting that Raz was low in mood and energy in session three, I stayed with what seemed like apathy as he slumped into the chair. I reminded him that I worked through the creative arts whenever it seemed appropriate, and suggested he might wish to consider using clay. Raz's expression at this suggestion was quite a sight to behold. He squirmed in the chair and pulled every imaginable face he could, all of which seemed to be categorising me, in no uncertain terms, as a real 'odd bod'!

Actually, given that Raz appeared quite lethargic I wondered what had prompted me to bring up the idea of using clay, since the physicality of the medium requires movement and some level of energy. Perhaps I was trying to locate the anger he had shown in the first two sessions? Possibly though, I had been moving too quickly; after his clear rejection of my idea, he took on a vacant look and his breathing slowed down considerably. I remained quiet, leaving the space and time for Raz to decide whether he wanted to talk or not, whether he wanted to use clay, or not.

The quietness and stillness in the room seemed significant and in the unhurried silence I became aware of a deep feeling of sadness. Knowing that I have an acute alertness to any young male's sadness, I needed to monitor my counter-transference. My emotional antennae could be hyperactive in these particular situations. Interestingly, there are times when a therapist's counter-transference can actually assist behind the scenes and, when Raz looked fully into my face, our eyes made contact and we experienced a moment of connection at a deeper level. By this I mean there appeared to be an unspoken understanding between us, something which it was not possible, or necessary to voice. Although my head may not have moved, I nevertheless felt as if I was discreetly nodding. I, too, had felt Raz's sadness.

'I feel a deep sense of sadness,' I said.

'Yeah,' came the reply.

I appreciate the slight nuances in facial expressions where so much is communicated in seconds. It is these moments when the ticking of the clock seems to hold a connection between individuals, and yet paradoxically time is suspended. I remember easing myself slowly forward in the chair and reaching over to the clay container, slowly removing the lid, and taking out a lump of clay. I placed the clay on a wooden board and rested the board on my knees, all in slow motion, nothing hurried. I had hoped my slow movements and slight tilt of the head towards Raz would be read as an invitation to join me.

And so it seemed, for he followed in taking some clay, and rested it on his own board. I wondered later if I had been coaxing him into some action too obviously. Perhaps there was a link here with the fact that Raz's parents had 'coaxed' him to move from London to East Anglia? Had my coaxing initially met with a reaction from Raz that related more to his earlier experience than our present time together?

There seemed no need to do anything with the clay, so I simply let it rest on the board; perhaps I was metaphorically 'holding' Raz? By now, Raz had made contact with his lump of clay and was pressing it down firmly on the board, making a flattened shape about the size of an A5 sketch pad. He looked up, announcing it was his iPad; a clay iPad, since he was not permitted to bring his own one from home into school.

'Well now, if it was for real and you switched it on, what would be on the screen?' I enquired.

Raz looked at the flattened clay and, seemingly unaware of what he was doing, carefully began to smooth the edges of the clay slab to make it look like a more stream-lined piece of information technology equipment. Mesmerised, he stared at the clay screen.

'Life's shit!' he said, with feeling.

Then he picked up a pencil and scratched into the clay. When he was nearly finished, he explained that the message he had etched was for his best friend telling him he would be returning to London soon. Taking up the idea, I enquired when this return would be — and did he know where he might live? There then followed a discussion that investigated how much of a reality returning to London could be.

It had been a session that took much energy out of me, as does any session where there is power in the feelings expressed. When Raz left, I reflected on what had been worked on but I did not identify the emotions in the room as integral to the grieving process, for to do so may have been an intrusion.

In the subsequent session Raz presented with a little more energy, sharing he had spoken with his parents about life and his studies after the examinations towards the end of the academic year. Clearly there was need for further discussion, and we explored the turbulence of adolescent years as young people try to work out what they want and what might be possible given their circumstances.

Raz, identified how unfair life can be for adolescents when they have no choice over what happens to them. We talked of desires and values in life and it seemed that he was asking about the 'meaning of life', looking for an answer to an existential question. Some might call it an existential crisis, although I did not feel Raz was reaching a crisis point, because he remained rational while attempting to work through the losses he had experienced in a situation beyond his control. Yes, he was low in mood; yes, at times he was angry; yes, at times he was philosophical, whilst underneath he was experiencing appropriate sadness. My part was to 'hold' his sadness, whilst he explored his feelings in our sessions together, so that he would not be consumed by an almighty anger that could threaten his chances in life as the age of only 16.

Our next session two weeks later was after a mid-term break at school. Raz spoke with enthusiasm of his visit to London during the break, when he had spent a few days staying with a friend at his home. The journey had been made by train and it was evident Raz had enjoyed travelling alone. He had enjoyed some independence and the time away from his family had given him an opportunity to see how life could be if and when he moved back to London on a semi-permanent basis to continue his education. I invited Raz to show me in clay, what he would look like in London. He laughed. I wondered if it was a laugh saying 'What?' Making full eye contact with Raz I encouraged him: 'Go on then!'

This time when Raz took a lump of clay I chose not to. I made the decision not to join him in using clay because he appeared emotionally stronger in the session and therefore it did not seem necessary for me to accompany him in the making process. Perhaps it was because I felt Raz held an ego strength that could cope with my tracking his process, and that he would be comfortable if I were to make observations while he worked in clay? As it turned out, my intuition that I should simply witness was correct.

With confidence Raz began to model a 'cool dude', as he called the figure taking shape in his hands. This clay character was given sturdy boots, a super-cool jacket and a cap. Raz worked carefully to make sure the figure could stand up on his own. He did this by firmly pressing the boots onto the wooden board; with further alterations to the lean and tilt of the figure Raz's creation needed no further support. I took this as a statement of self-affirmation. I could see by the slight smile on Raz's face

Cool Dude

that he was pleased with his clay model. He took a deep breath.
  'Finished!'
  'I can see he is finished. Tell me about him.'
This may seem rather directive in terms of adolescent therapy,
but my experience proves that if a young person genuinely
does not wish to do something, there is no way that any of my
half-whispered invitations or suggestions will encourage them
in that direction.
  'Well, well. Well you can see what he's like — he knows what
he's about. He knows what he's doing!' stated Raz.
  I nodded.

'He's just coming back from college. He's me next September when I'm at college in London.'

'Ah! He looks okay,' I responded.

'Yeah, he'll be just fine, he will,' Raz said.

The remainder of the session was taken up with Raz telling me in detail about his recent trip to London. I was curious about what arrangements would be made by Raz and his family for him to attend college in London, but reminded myself I did not need to know such minutiae. Raz concluded by saying he did not feel he needed to come to therapy much more because he felt different. We agreed to meet for a final session the following week.

In the concluding session I asked Raz what he needed to happen to his clay works. He was uncertain and said he would think about it as we worked. I then tentatively suggested that he might, perhaps, make the Raz of 'today' in clay. He was thoughtful for a while, then reached for some clay and a wooden board. I accompanied Raz with taking some clay myself, almost as if in the position of a mother saying her 'goodbyes' to her son who was leaving for college, whilst also recognising this could be seen as the last part of the 'holding' process. I surmised that I might be working through counter-transference for I, too, had a son who had left home a few years earlier.

Raz began to model a clay figure and I observed from the sidelines, working my own piece of clay. Today's figure was not quite as sturdy as the 'London Raz' and, when I looked down at what my hands had fashioned I could see I had made a rough chair.

'I think I've made a chair today,' I said to Raz.

'What for?' questioned Raz.

'Not sure ... I know! This chair is for Raz to use whilst doing homework and waiting to move to London,' I offered.

Giving an almost coy smile, Raz took my clay chair and worked at seating his figure in it.

'I'd like to take my clay figures home with me,' he said.

'Of course,' I affirmed.

Our work was done. When Raz left the last session I smiled to myself. I was sad to see him go, for I had enjoyed working with him, but felt satisfied we had covered what he had needed to work through. Although he had initially presented as an angry adolescent, when there had been time to express his frustrations at being powerless I had begun to see the fine young person I had had the privilege to work alongside. Sometimes it is hard for the therapist to see a client leave, but it is so right.

Discussion

The referral had been received from a concerned class teacher. In Raz's case there was a clear focus to the therapeutic work in the short-term contract we had both agreed on and this was appropriate. When our contract came to a close, I hoped Raz would be successful in his desire to return to London.

The therapeutic work had centred on the theme of sometimes holding and sometimes letting go; a classic theme. It was as if the mother and baby had been together and the time had come for the child to separate, transitioning to independence. The therapy theme had echoed the family theme.

Writing this final case study had been so apt, for a therapist working with children and adolescents must eventually always let go of children and adolescents, who initially were troubled, and watch as they move back into the outside world. The cutting of the metaphorical umbilical cord reverberates, hitting a profoundly sacred chord.

And what you thought you came for is only a shell, a husk of meaning
From which the purpose breaks only when it is fulfilled.

T. S. Eliot, Four Quartets, '*Little Gidding*', 1944

PART FOUR

CLAY THERAPY INITIATIVES

CHAPTER 16

Recent Research into the
Use of Clay Therapy

Research into clay therapy has been gathering momentum over the last few years. This chapter takes an overview of five master's level dissertations. Four were produced by students participating in the Academy of Play and Child Psychotherapy (APAC) MA in Practice-Based Play Therapy in collaboration with Canterbury Christ Church University. The fifth dissertation was written by a student from Cambridge University.

Each has its own merit, offering innovative insights and demonstrates growing interest in the therapeutic use of clay. It is not a new way of working, but has not been widely written about, hence the invaluable inclusion of the studies. Many professionals say that they have used clay in therapy sessions before, but have never been sure what to do with the process, nor understood completely what has been taking place. This chapter should be a welcome addition to the scant literature on clay therapy.

Eileen Braham, 2012

Master's Dissertation Title:
To study the use of clay in a series of therapy sessions with primary school boys of African heritage who demonstrate symptoms of oppositional defiance.

Eileen Braham explained that her professional practice for the past twenty years had involved working both therapeutically and non-therapeutically with vulnerable children. As a qualified play therapist she recognised children's behaviours stem from their experiences in the early years of life, when emotional and physical needs were not met, or where inappropriate expectations and demands had been placed on them. Braham shared her view that the harsh and inconsistent experiences the children were subjected to meant many of those she worked with struggled to verbally express themselves. She subsequently discovered the medium of clay was an aid to emotional expression.

The intent of Braham's dissertation was to evaluate the use of clay therapy with 8- to 9-year-old boys of African Heritage. The research participants lived in an area of high social deprivation in the south-east of England. These boys exhibited symptoms of oppositional disorder behaviour in classroom settings, but had not been diagnosed ODB according to the *Diagnostic and Statistical Manual of Mental Disorder,* (4th edn). The DSM-1V-TR, (2000) identifies ODB as a pattern of persistently negativistic, hostile, defiant behaviour lasting at least six months, during which four (or more) of the following are present:

+ Often looses temper
+ Often argues with adults
+ Often actively defies or refuses to comply with adults requests or rules
+ Often deliberately annoys people
+ Often blames others for his or her mistakes or misbehaviour

+ Is often touchy or easily annoyed by others
+ Is often angry and resentful
+ Is spiteful or vindictive

Discovering it was virtually impossible to uncover any research undertaken using clay therapy with boys of African heritage who demonstrated symptoms of ODB in the classroom Braham's research theme aimed to:

+ Evaluate the effectiveness of clay therapy on boys demonstrating oppositional disorder behaviour in the classroom.
+ Indentify any changes in oppositional disorder behaviour displayed by the boys in the classroom during the course of the study.

The study offered fourteen, individual, weekly, non-directive sessions of 30 to 35 minutes, during which participants freely worked with clay. Braham studied carefully how the participants made initial contact with the clay, how they manipulated the medium, how their movements changed and whether there were any noticeable changes to the participants' breathing patterns. To record this data Braham devised the Braham Sensory Indicator which she completed for each research session with all participants giving her 84 data sets.

Further data was gathered by using the following:

+ An independent advisor, educator and clinician experienced in Jungian theory evaluated the clay creations/processes focusing on metaphor and symbolism.
+ Kinetic-House-Tree-Person (K-H-T-P) (Burns, 1987) diagagnostic drawing at the start, mid-point and end of the research process.
+ Sutter Eyberg Teacher Behaviour Inventory — Revised Scale, (1999) completed weekly thus providing an evaluation of the participant's behaviour after each session.

This hermeneutic study emphasized the interpretive dialogue between the researcher, clay images, K-H-T-P drawings and the SESBI-R questionnaires, whilst also accepting the inevitable influences of personal, cultural and historical biases. (McNiff, 2004) Braham discovered that her young research participants made clay creations along similar themes to that of the 100 adults in the research carried out between 2007 and 2009 (Souter-Anderson, 2010).

Creations of people and human forms were significant themes, followed by a second theme depicting the earth's elements. Reporting that participants all held the clay before starting to work with it, Braham explained the touching stimulated a type of chain reaction where nerve endings in the fingertips were sending messages directly to the brain (Souter-Anderson, 2010). Impulses were then fed back through the fingers and hands which resulted in movement.

The deeper breathing Braham noticed in her study occurred when participants were in the manipulation and forming stage of working with clay and before completing the sculpts. She suggests this possibly meant that as the participants engaged fully with the creating process they were working at a deeper emotional level in silence where there was direct communication with the psyche.

Braham reported participants expressed some strong emotion in the form of anger, but that working with the clay enabled the energy and anger to be expressed in a safe manner. Interestingly, Braham recorded notions of personal identity pervaded the clay creations. As identity developed, self-esteem increased and the boys were able to start viewing themselves and their culture more positively. By the end of the study, analysis of the data evidenced a 50% improvement in the participants' behaviour. This then pointed to the value of using clay therapy with boys of African heritage showing symptoms of ODB.

However, Braham raised a number of questions that are worthy of consideration:

✦ Was the duration of the study period long enough to effect change? For two participants this clearly was not the case and further therapeutic intervention was offered.

✦ Would the use of another questionnaire such as Goodman's Strength and Difficulties questionnaire provide a clearer picture to the difficulties in behaviour being demonstrated by the participants?

✦ Would the results have been similar with a different cultural group or gender?

✦ Would results have been different if clay themes had been implemented?

In conclusion, Braham stated the research demonstrated there were benefits to using clay with boys showing symptoms of ODB. Offering clay therapy potentially can provide support to many clients with a wide range of emotional and behaviour challenges.

Caroline Drew, 2012

Master's Dissertation Title:
An evaluation of specific behaviour patterns following a series of group clay sessions with boys aged ten years old exhibiting symptomology of dyslexia and displaying oppositional defiant behaviours in the classroom.

This small-scale, qualitative, systematic hermeneutic study was supported by quantitative data evaluating the effects of using non-directive clay sessions of 45 minutes with a group of six boys aged 10 years with two facilitators, over a 12-week period. All participants were Caucasian, living in two parent, mid-range socio-economic group families. The research question asked, 'Could working with clay as a therapeutic modality help boys integrate more effectively into the classroom and become more task- focused?'

The children were instructed to use 8cms cubes of natural, greyish coloured clay in any way they wanted to. For assessment purposes, the researcher used the following:

✦ Research observation sheets with an in dependent clay supervisor's notes supported by symbolic consideration.
✦ Drew Attitude Assessment Scale (DAAS-Researcher construct, 2012).
✦ Goodman's Strength and Difficulties Questionnaire (SDQ: 1987).

Analysis of the research data indicated all boys showed a great deal of improvement initially in several areas of classroom learning. The final results revealed the group therapeutic clay sessions evidenced symbolic manifestations through the clay creations, demonstrating good engagement in the process with the boys undergoing some transitional change, subconsciously and consciously. The clay stories showed the children had been able to project issues and concerns they had onto the clay, accepting and owning these within a supportive group environment.

Susannah Bradley, 2012

Master's Dissertation Title:
To evaluate the effects of a series of clay therapy sessions on girls aged between 8 and 9 demonstrating symptoms of generalised anxiety disorder, as defined in the DSM-IV TR section 300.02, in a classroom setting.

Susannah Bradley's initial interest in the use of clay in therapy began whilst training to become a play therapist. She experienced working with clay as the medium which had the greatest impact on her personally, explaining that it helped to work at a much deeper emotional level. As Bradley's training progressed so did the use of clay with the children in her clinical placement, particularly when working with girls struggling with anxiety.

Wishing to explore this phenomena further, Bradley devised an MA research proposal using a series of clay therapy sessions with girls aged from 8- to 9-years-old showing symptoms of generalised anxiety disorder in a classroom setting. All participants were Caucasian, attended the same school, and were from a low socio-economic group. Each girl lived with her biological mother, siblings and mother's partner.

Children with generalised anxiety disorder may be overly conforming, perfectionist and unsure of themselves. They may need to redo tasks because of excessive dissatisfaction with a less than perfect performance. They may be typically over zealous in seeking approval and need excessive reassurance about their performance and other worries.

Bradley's hermeneutic study aimed to:

a) assess if there were any changes in how (the participants) expressed themselves through their work with clay;

b) assess whether working with this medium resulted in observable changes in the behaviour of the participants in the classroom environment;

c) identify changes in the indicators of anxiety displayed by the participants whilst at school; and

d) identify any changes in how the participants engaged with
    their teachers and their peer group.

Each participant attended twelve weekly clay therapy sessions of
40 minutes duration. Hand-size lumps of clay, wooden boards,
water, modelling tools and rolling pins were provided for the
participants who were given a theme to work to, this being
stated at the start of each research session. The themes covered
how the participants experienced significant people and places
(Who am I? mother, father, siblings, home and school) in their
daily lives. The six themes were repeated twice during the
twelve- week research programme.

Data was collected using Goodman's Strength and Difficulties
Questionnaires (SDQ; 1987) a Screen for Anxiety-related Emotional
Disorders Questionnaire (SCARED; 1999). An independent clay
therapist evaluated the clay creations.

It was noteworthy that when analysing the 72 data sets only
sixteen different categories of images were identified. Seventeen
per cent were predominantly of a person, 12 per cent were cube
shapes, 11 per cent represented food and 8 per cent were animal
creations. This data linked to the fact that children aged around
8 and 9 years old generally draw, paint or make that which they
know and are familiar with. Abstract representations are a little
too sophisticated for this age group.

Given the stated themes, it was not surprising that models
of people ranked highest in the created images. However, the
making of many cubes is curious. Cubes resemble precise,
geometric shapes, perhaps indicating a need to be in control, or
of something needing to be perfect in appearance. This may have
been indicative of the research participants trying to keep hold of
anxieties experienced, because to experience them in the external
world may have been too much for them to cope with. This could
suggest the need for the participant to work through personal
anxieties alone.

It is understandable that food was also a dominant theme in
the clay creations. Here there were indications of the high level of

importance attached to nourishment, nurture and the nurturing environment for the participants. The animals created in clay took the form of pets such as cats and dogs. These animals were reported to be a focus for the child's affection or their own need for affection.

Bradley noted the way participants handled the clay. Each participant discovered her own technique of manipulating and moulding the clay as she became more familiar with the researcher, medium and environment. Red- and grey-coloured clays on offer were used by all participants and in some instances the two different coloured clays were blended together. The researcher suggested participants had the ability to discriminate in their knowledge, and that at times boundaries were blurred and at other times they merged and came together as one, or that sometimes one could be more dominant to another.

Acknowledging that it was challenging work to understand and evaluate the clay creations, Bradley appreciated the clinical supervision as much as the academic supervision since she was occupying the role of an 'insider researcher', which may become problematic when research participants get in touch with buried feelings and some raw emotions surfaced. She offered that the clay images appeared to tell stories for each child. In some cases the participants regressed to exploring the medium using infantile actions, as opposed to developmentally age-appropriate actions. However, all participants were proud of their creations even though some strong negative emotions had been experienced.

Analysis of the gathered data showed the research had been effective in lessening anxiety levels for four of the six girls at the end of the study, although at a mid-term point in the life of the research all six girls were showing a reduction in anxiety symptoms. Importantly though, all of Goodman's Strength and Difficulty scores had improved. Teachers involved with the study shared the view that all participants had benefited from taking part and that the girls' behaviour within the classroom environment had changed. By the end of the study the participants were;

✦   answering more questions,
✦   not needing always to be near an adult in the classroom,
✦   asserting themselves with peers in situations they might
      not have done so previously, both in the playground and
      in the classroom,
✦   participating actively in the end-of-year assembly.

Whilst the research was limited in size and specific in age, gender, ethnicity and social grouping, this nevertheless does not detract from the value of the study that evidences working therapeutically with clay can reduce anxiety levels in girls aged 8 to 9. Bradley concludes her dissertation by offering:

The researcher believes there is still so much for her to learn about clay therapy and the journey is really just beginning even though this piece of research is over. Clay is a very powerful medium, working on levels that are difficult to access by any other medium.

Donna Jones, 2013

M.Ed. Research Title:
Is making pottery on iPads therapeutic? Exploring children's
feedback about their play experience.

In introducing her study, Donna Jones describes personal experience of contact with clay and with an iPad, suggesting both offer a cool, smooth feel and are affected through touch. Her interest in a meeting point between clay and touch-screen sensation was activated further when she became aware of pottery applications for touch screens, including one with options for three-dimensional printing. Jones wondered how children would report their experience of making pottery on iPad screens and if this activity was potentially therapeutic.

In the study children aged between 4 and 11 attending a school holiday club were invited to be co-researchers or 'clay detectives', investigating their own experience of making virtual pottery on iPads. Real clay, tools and a small wheel were also offered in the setting so that children had a contrast for their explorations. Consent and assent were received for 29 children. During two half-day sessions 26 children chose to play with one or both media. Twenty-two chose to complete a simple smiley-face questionnaire, and 10 to use an audio recorder to capture their findings as they played. Children then used iPads to capture images of their virtual and real clay creations. Photographs were taken of children at play, being careful to ensure anonymity.

The study found the majority of children present in the setting chose to engage with both real clay and virtual pottery, and that those who gave feedback offered positive reports of both play experiences. Children appeared to move easily from one to the other and sometimes back again. The creative play experience using iPads proved sociable bringing children together rather than separating them, as did play around tables with real clay. iPads appeared to offer children across the age range a creative tool that they could quickly master. Several children also chose to work with real clay on the small pottery wheel provided.

In relation to virtual pottery play, children were very satisfied by the appearance of their finished work and enjoyed colouring, decorating and the process of firing virtual pottery which evoked expressions of delight in some. Imaginations were activated with roles and representations given by children to their creations, just as they were with real clay. Virtual pottery play produced many uniquely decorated vessels with and without lids, but one child was able to shape a volcano and a UFO instead. Two thirds of clay creations were open containers such as pots or bowls, but a third were not: for example, one child made a tiger in a cave.

Children indicated that real clay and virtual clay were alike and also very different, and described how real clay could be made sticky, pulled apart, dropped or have a hole made in it. Photographs of children at play and their comments suggested that they contacted real clay in a greater range of ways, according to how they used their own bodies and applied water and tools, but that certain action gestures, such as fingertip smoothing and pressing, occurred often in both media. Jones suggests that both processes may sit on the same haptic continuum.

Jones wondered if virtual clay may have disadvantages for children wanting fuller, three-dimensional contact, but offer advantages in settings where clay cannot be used: for example when children are physically weakened by illness, very low in confidence or sensitive to heavy and messy materials due to trauma. Such predictable and gentle embodied experiences may act as a bridge to fuller contact with clay over time.

Findings from the study suggest that making virtual pottery on iPads may be therapeutic for children by offering opportunity for enjoyment, achievement and through activation of the imagination. Jones however noted that her research did not reveal whether the sculpting and painting of clay on a touch screen can activate the types of soothing or relaxant effects that real clay can.

Louise Burton, 2013

Master's Dissertation Title:
Bringing the outside in. an exploration of the playful use of clay and natural materials on the self-esteem of young children.

The purpose of the research project was to find whether a clay and natural material-based intervention could help to reduce the impact of nature-deficiency, which potentially leads to children suffering long-term developmental consequences, such as reduced self-esteem in young children. Interestingly, the results collated later found that a natural materials-based intervention could also positively affect other areas of development and emotional behaviour.

The sample included five children aged between 8 and 9 years old from the same primary school. Eight individual sessions took place in a play therapy room, which was laid out to represent a natural environment and to encapsulate feelings of being in nature. Clay and a wide selection of natural materials were provided for the children to explore. This included pieces of wood and bark, twigs, stones, shells, feathers, pine cones, a selection of foliage, moss, leaves, flowers and other interesting found materials. The children were invited to play as they desired. The study had been designed with the child's voice in mind, in line with a phenomenological approach.

The primary research method used to evaluate the effectiveness of the sessions was the Butler's Self Image Profile for Children (SIP-C; 2001) completed by the children in the sample before and after the intervention. A second means of evaluating other changes brought about as a result of the intervention was the Goodman's Strength and Difficulties Questionnaire (SDQ; 1987) completed by the class teachers in the pre-, mid-point and post-research sessions. Finally, to observe and record the children's process and feelings throughout the sessions, the researcher devised and used the Researcher Observation Sheet (ROS). These sheets, along with photographs of the images each child created, were reviewed by a clay specialist who offered her clinical input.

According to Burton the participants' confidence in using the materials became apparent as the sessions progressed, with the children sharing excitement at their achievements. Clay is known for its malleable qualities and any 'mistakes' can be easily rectified. Souter-Anderson (2010) talks about how clay can be moulded and altered which leaves the maker free to change emerging images and discoveries. It seemed that the natural materials enhanced the images, making them bolder and brighter, inspiring the participants to become more adventurous in their creations. The red clay was noted to be the more popular choice of clay, whilst the overwhelming favourite natural materials used by the children were feathers, shells and wood. Burton notes these popular materials represent the four elements; clay (earth), feathers (air), shells (water), and wood (fire) relaying Turner's (2005) suggestion that the elements constitute the basic template of material existence. They are perceived as informing or giving character to the 'stuff' of life.

One participant described the sensation that he would get in his body whilst sculpting in clay saying, 'When I touch the clay I get a tingly feeling. I feel it in the middle of my spine — it's like when I feel cold, it's a nice feeling.' Another participant had never seen clay, nor had any experience of playing with natural materials, especially in his early years spent in Eastern Europe. He became very inquisitive during the sessions and would ask questions about the names and origins of the materials. He became fascinated with the clay, wanting to smell it, smooth it, manipulate it, to discover more about it. It seemed that possibly this experience had ignited a new-found-love for nature, an innate love that Wilson (1984) suggests humans all possess.

Results showed an improvement in both the children's self-esteem and their self-image, as well as improvements in their concentration and emotional well-being. In conclusion the data indicated how playfully exploring clay and natural materials in a safe therapeutic space was an effective means of supporting and enhancing children's self-esteem and perception of self, as well carrying the potential to assist working through some challenging emotions. Moreover, Burton was told how many of the creations had taken pride of place at home in the children's bedrooms. This lead the researcher to believe the sculpts may have held a special meaning for the children, perhaps becoming a transitional object.

Summary

What four of the above research studies demonstrate is that with different client bases the use of clay in therapy was worthwhile for the children who were participants. Outcomes showed concentration was increased, self-esteem rose and general behaviour improved. The dissertation involving iPads evidenced that both real and virtual clay were appreciated by participants. From these small-scale studies, pointers therefore highlight the value of using the primordial substance of clay to enhance the quality of emotional and behavioural lives of many children and adolescents. The theoretical underpinning of clay therapy known as 'A theory of contact: physical, emotional, spiritual and metaphorical' truly is a theory about making contact with the self and all that entails along the journey. It is a theory that touches the experience of every individual and it deals with making meaning and gaining understanding, concepts at the very core of working with clay.

✽ ✽ ✽ ✽ ✽

Clay therapy is still a developing field, consequently emerging studies of this nature are enormously valuable in providing knowledge and skill building to improve practice in child and adolescent therapeutic domains.

CHAPTER 17

Specialist Training Programmes in using Clay: Clay Conversations, Clay Therapy & Supervision of Clay Therapy & Conversations

Introduction

With the reprinting of this book in 2024, an ideal opportunity has presented itself to bring this chapter up to date.

Interest in the therapeutic use of clay has grown considerably during the past decade, with requests for an online clay course and a specialist clinical supervision training to be made available. A progression route is now in place for working with clay when the intention is to support others with enhancing well-being. This also means there now exist further courses for therapists to broaden and deepen their skills when using clay as a therapeutic medium in sessions.

The first stage in the training programme is the online Practitioner Award in Clay Conversations written at a postgraduate level for those interested in offering well-being support. Upon completion of this initial training, many practitioners have a desire to progress further and train to become a Clay Therapist, thereby enabling them to work with clay therapeutically with more complex emotional troubles. The third and final stage in the progression route is the Clay Therapy and Conversations Specialist Supervision course that provides a comprehensive in-depth consideration when working with clay, to give form to unrecognised and unspoken concerns.

The three training programmes are considered in further detail below.

Stage One - Practitioner Award in Clay Conversations

The Practitioner Award in Clay Conversations was written as a direct response to requests for help in supporting children, adolescents, adults, and senior members within communities, as the restrictions from the Coronavirus disease (COVID-19) pandemic eased.

These requests came from community-minded people who were seeking to use clay as a means of supporting others who were struggling with a sense of well-being — the requests came from different countries around the world which meant considering novel and creative ideas in the writing of a training programme. What emerged was a unique and innovative online course offering an integrative approach to clay work, play, and modelling, interwoven with active listening skills in a live, interactive small-group forum.

The Clay Conversations training programme was created with the purpose of using clay to work, play or sculp whilst talking and sharing whatever comes into mind. This relaxed approach is helpful in supporting well-being when holding the space for others and validating their clay workings through thoughtful responses.

Clay Conversations settings are referred to as 'meetings' as opposed to 'sessions', to denote the difference between the intention to support well-being and that of Clay Therapy. However, there is likely to be a therapeutic element to working with clay in general, whatever the setting, as evidenced by the author's research. (Souter-Anderson, 2012) Further details may be obtained from the website www.clayconversations.org

Stage Two - Clay Therapy Training

The second stage in the progression route is the Clay Therapy training, which is simply so much more than learning new techniques, skills and interventions. The work here focuses on the therapists and their core theoretical practice, whilst enabling experiences to be seen with the heart and felt through the body when connecting with the client in discovering where the therapeutic work is needed. The course engages participants in an in-depth exploration of many theoretical concepts covering object-relations theory, Jungian theory as well as Existential perspectives.

This course was initially designed in 2012 for qualified therapeutic practitioners who have completed their own respective training as a creative arts therapist, play therapist, counsellor or psychotherapist. The Clay Therapy training continues to be enhanced with updated content every few years. The course content is likely to appeal also to art therapists, sandplay therapists, authentic movement therapists and music therapists. Clay therapy enrichment events follow on from the course. Further details may be obtained from the Clay Therapy website. www.claytherapy.co.uk

Specialist Clinical Supervision Training in
Clay Therapy and Conversations

There remains a growing need for clinical supervisors trained in the specialist fields of Clay Therapy and Clay Conversations and this was identified by advanced Clay Therapy practitioners. To meet the needs of these experienced therapists a new training course was created in 2022. This Specialist Clinical Supervision Training in Clay Therapy and Conversations was written to Level 7, RQF guidelines (Regulated Qualification Framework, UK) and equips and enables advanced practitioners to support and guide Clay Therapists and Clay Conversationists in their work with clay. The training program provides a wholesome and solid foundation in this specialist field and adopts a collegiate approach to support and guide therapists in deepening clay craft and emotional development, both in self and for others.

The specialist supervision course is suitable for counsellors, psychotherapists, play therapists, psychologists and clinical supervisors who already hold the Advanced Clay Therapy Award and, who also have a minimum of 5 years-experience, as a therapeutic professional.

❄ ❄ ❄ ❄ ❄

Clay Conversations www.clayconversations.org Clay Therapy www.claytherapy.co.uk and the Specialist Clinical Supervision in Clay Therapy and Conversations, are associated branches of the Clay Therapy and Clay Conversations Community with trainings being offered under the auspices of Bridging Creative Therapies Consultancy www.bctconsultancy.co.uk

APPENDIX

A Theory of Contact:
Physical, Emotional, Spiritual and Metaphorical

The Five Lens Framework for Clay Therapy Theory
(Souter-Anderson, 2010, p. 52)

Lens 1: Making contact
Lens 2: Play space of potential
Lens 3: Clay play in the presence of another
Lens 4: Bridging space of potential
Lens 5: Emerging theme

Lens 1: Making contact

When touching clay we are making contact with the prima materia and therefore we are working with the very matter that we are made from, so deeply are we connected to the earth. It could be said that we are in touch with our primal Self — our very inner core and true Self. When this is happening rigidity of thinking is suspended as we move into a state of flux, because we are metaphorically touching the medium that is the beginning of all things; clay as earth is the root of existence (Jung, Schwartz-Salant (ed.), 1995).

Lens 2: Play space of potential

Clay therapy is essentially a sensorimotor experience, centring on touch. Touch is a fundamental sense to human experience and existence and is associated with arousal and libido instinct (Freud, 1908) where feeling and sensing merge.

The play space of potential is a truly integrative stage, in which the physical, physiological, neurological and neuro-chemical dimensions are synthesising the experiences of the client as clay is being worked with. There are so many levels and connections as the inner and outer worlds of the client come together with the inner and outer worlds of the therapist, and transformational experiences are made possible through the therapeutic relationship.

The impact on the therapist should not be forgotten, for indeed just as the client is affected, so too is the therapist, because of being in such close proximity to the physical being of the client and the work in hand. This is the point at which the importance of the therapist's self-awareness and felt sense of what they are experiencing through the work is an essential component of the process, informing them in their search for meaning.

At the core of lens 2 are four fundamental dimensions:

1   touch and fingertip massage
2   movement
3   breath
4   altered states of consciousness

All highly significant when contained within the therapist's emotional 'holding' capacity. Each dimension is explained below.

Touch and Fingertip massage

Blakeslee and Blakeslee (2007) chart the journey of touch through the peri-personal sphere, offering a correlation between the meaning of touch and ownership of what is being touched. This link helps to establish the significance and extension of Self to whatever is being made in clay, that is to say, 'I made this. This is me'. (Souter-Anderson, 2010, p. 59)

Here, a sense of omnipotence points the way to personal significance. This is given further credence when considering the multitude of nerve endings housed in the fingertips are trans-mitting thousands of signals to the brain through the sensation of touch. When this is happening the neuroplasticity of the brain is capable of creating new neural pathways, thereby potentially restructuring previously held views and beliefs. Personal thought patterns create an ongoing narrative, enabling the client to give voice and expression to feelings that hitherto have been difficult to express. All this happens through the hands touching the clay: that is to say, the hands and fingertips tell the story.

Movement

Whether the client is seated or standing, as the hands or other parts of the body come into contact with the clay the diaphragm also moves. As the clay is manipulated and worked on, the client's body finds a movement rhythm that stimulates the potential of releasing repressed material. If the diaphragm is able to move reasonably freely, the therapeutic work is able to go deep due to the fact that this muscle massages our internal organs, releasing suppressed feelings (Boyesen, 1970).

Breath

When we breathe more deeply, therefore more slowly, emotional states are capable of being calmed. Common to all life (human, animal, or vegetable) is the need for oxygen or the 'breath of life', whose movement into the organism is essential and was referred to by Ridley (2006) as the 'Long tide'. Working with clay offers an experience of relaxation that suggests a form of self-regulation, accompanied by a sense of calm potentially resulting in a process of self-soothing. Relaxation eases tension, which in turn can often enable verbal expression of feelings because the mind is freed to make associations.

Altered state of consciousness

When closely observing the client's facial expressions and monitoring their breathing it is noticeable that the client can move into an altered state of consciousness, similar at times to being in a trance-like state or when meditating. Some might describe this condition as perhaps mystical or even as an 'oceanic feeling' (Freud, 1929), and this brings us full circle to the evolutionary thinking that is described in lens 1.

However, it is worth remembering that whilst it is possible that clients may appear to 'surrender to the clay' and be working in an altered state of consciousness during some of their clay work, they may also spend much of the time working at what appears to be a more a conscious level. For example, 'I'm making us some dinner', or 'This is a flower'. Such are the different states of consciousness and awareness operating in tandem.

Lens 3: Clay Play in the presence of another

During clay work the client and therapist become linked inter-psychically with the intuitive attentiveness of the therapist helping to progress the work. This is the critical emotional 'holding' phase; sensitivity and receptivity are enhancing all that is flowing in the moment. The fluidity of the moment fosters an illusion of 'oneness'. Such is the degree of togetherness, which is akin to the 'primary maternal preoccupation' (Winnicott, 1964) when a newborn is completely encircled by the physical and emotional presence of the mother during the first few weeks of the baby's life.

Whilst the above is progressing at a neurochemical level, so much is happening as the body responds to these pleasurable emotional and metaphorical 'holding' experiences, resulting in increased levels of endorphins being released. Here the inter-connectedness and intra-connectedness — for both client and therapist — is experienced with increased concentration, absorption and vibrancy; here there is fusion in minds.

What transpires through the play in the presence of another is a transformational process, as thoughts and ideas percolate and transmute. However, on a very practical level sometimes the therapist's involvement may be more direct as children often invite the therapist to assist in their clay creations. Such experiences of co-creation provide important opportunities for relationship building.

Lens 4: Bridging Space of Potential

A second space of significance exists between lens 4 and lens 5. Holding in mind that in Jungian terms the relationship is the 'vessel', within the 5-lens diagram we see that there is a conical vase-shape between lens 4 and 5, reminiscent of the early alchemists' equipment for changing a base material or metal into gold, a process they called alchemy. In clay therapy this alchemy occurs when the client's imagination, stimulated in the right hemisphere of the brain, connects via the corpus callosum with the left cognitive hemisphere of the brain, resulting in the possibility of new meaning being created. The fourth lens has been named the 'bridging space of potential', because something from the client's internal world has connected with the outer world. When it is sensed and felt in the heart, some therapists have described the experience as a spiritual and/or metaphorical one.

The bridging space of potential is heightened when the therapist is fully working through the four avenues of exploration; the case study in Chapter 13, 'Eating Conditions: Libby (age 14)'. Provides an example of how this may occur in a therapeutic situation.

Lens 5: Emerging theme

In lens 5 the work moves into a refining process of transmuting information through the newly created narrative when different perspectives offer new understanding with the help of the therapist's 'containing' presence. Existential themes; sometimes referred to as the 'treasure' (or new understanding) emerge from this transformational process and potentially, is likely to relate to an aspect of the client's physical, social, personal or spiritual presence in the world (van Deurzen and Arnold-Baker, 2005).

I recommend readers consult chapter three of *Touching Clay, Touching What? The Use of Clay in Therapy* (Souter-Anderson, 2010) for a full and detailed explanation of the development of a theory to explain the workings of clay therapy.

BIBLIOGRAPHY

American Psychiatric Association, 2000 *Diagnostic and Statistical Manual of Mental Health Disorders (DSM-IV-TR)*, American Psychiatric Association, Arlington VA.

Bion, W.R., 1970, *Attention and Interpretation*. Karnac Books, London.

Birmaher B., Brent D.A., Chiappetta L., Bridge J., Monga S., and Baugher M., 1999. 'Psychometric properties of the Screen for Child Anxiety Related Emotional Disorders (SCARED): A Replication Study'. *Journal of the American Academy of Child and Adolescent Psychiatry, 38, pp.1230-6.*

Blakeslee, S. & Blakeslee, M., 2007, *The Body has a Mind of its Own*. Random House, New York.

Boyesen, G., 1970, 'Experiences with Dynamic Relaxation'. *Energy and Character 1(1)*, PP 11-20; reprinted 1980 in *The Collected Papers of Biodynamic Psychology 1*, Biodynamic Psychology Publications, London.

Bradley, S., 2012 'To evaluate the effects of a series of clay therapy sessions on girls aged between 8 and 9 demonstrating symptoms of generalised anxiety disorder, as defined in the DSM-IV-TR section 300.02, in a classroom setting.' *Unpublished Master's dissertation.* Canterbury Christchurch University, UK.

Braham, E., 2012, 'To study the use of clay in a series of therapy sessions with primary school boys of African heritage who demonstrate symptoms of oppositional defiance.' *Unpublished Master's dissertation.* Canterbury Christchurch University, UK.

Burns, R.C., 1987, *Kinetic-House-Tree-Person Drawings (K-H-T-P): An Interpretative Manual*. Brunner-Routledge, London.

Burton, L., 2013, 'Bringing the outside in: an exploration of the playful use of clay and natural materials on the self-esteem of young children.' *Unpublished Master's dissertation.* Canterbury Christchurch University, UK.

Butler, R. J., 2001, *The Self Image Profile for Children (SIP-C) and Adolescents (SIP-A).* Pearson Assessment, London.

Casement P., 1985. *On Learning from the Patient.* Tavistock Publications Ltd., London.

Drew, C., 2012, 'An evaluation of specific behaviour patterns following a series of group clay sessions with boys aged ten years old exhibiting symptomology of dyslexia, and displaying oppositional defiant behaviours in the classroom.' *Unpublished Master's dissertation.* Canterbury Christchurch University, UK.

Eliot, T.S., 1944, *Four Quartets.* Faber & Faber Ltd, London.

Erikson, E., 1967, *Childhood and Society.* Standard edition 9, Penguin, Middlesex.

Freud, S., (1908) 1961, *On the Sexual Theories of Children.* Standard edition 9, Hogarth Press, 1961, London.

Freud, S., (1917) 1955, *Mourning and Melancholia. XV11* 2nd edn, Hogarth Press, London.

Freud, S., (1929) 1961, *Civilization and its Discontent.* Standard edition 21, Hogarth Press, London.

Goodman, R., 1987, 'The Strengths and Difficulties Questionaire: A Research Note', *Journal of Child Psychology & Psychiatry,* 38, 581 – 586.

Jones, D., 2013, 'Is making pottery on iPads therapeutic? Exploring children's feedback about their play experience.' *Unpublished Master's dissertation*, Cambridge University, UK.

Jung, C.G., 1995, *Jung on Alchemy*, Schwartz-Salant, N. (ed.), Routledge, London.

McNiff, S., 2004, *Art Heals: How Creativity Cures the Soul.* Shamhbala Publications Ltd., Massachusetts.

Piaget, J., 1962, *Play, Dreams and Imitations.* Norton, New York.

Piaget, J. 1971, *Psychology and Epistomology: Towards a Theory of Knowledge*, A. Rosin (trans) Viking, New York.

Ridley, C. 2006, *Stillness: Biodynamic Cranial Practice and the Evolution of Consciousness.* North Atlantic Books, California.

Souter-Anderson, L., 2010, *Touching Clay, Touching What? The Use of Clay in Therapy.* Archive Publishing, Dorset.

Souter-Anderson, L., 2019, *Seeking Shelter, Seeking Safety: Clay Therapy with Families and Groups.* Archive Publishing, Dorset.

Stevens, A., 1990, *On Jung.* Routledge, London

Sutter Eyberg, S., 1999, *Sutter Eyberg Student Behavior Inventory.* Psychological Assessment Resources, Lutz, Florida.

Turner, B. A., 2005, *The Handbook of Sandplay Therapy.* Temenos Press, California.

Van Deurzen, E. & Arnold-Baker, C. (eds), 2005, *Existential Perspectives on Human Issues: a Handbook for Therapeutic Practice.* Sage Publications, London.

Wells, H.G., (1911) 2004, *Floor Games. A Father's Account of Play and its Legacy of Healing*, Turner B. (ed.), Temenos Press, California.

Wilson, E. O., 1984, *Biophilia: The Human Bond with Other Species.* Harvard University Press, Cambridge.

Winnicott, D.W., 1964, *The Child, The Family and The Outside World.* Penguin, Middlesex.

Winnicott, D. W., 1971, *Playing and Reality.* Routledge, London.

INDEX